PENGUIN BOOKS

LIFELINES

LIFELINES

An Anthology of Poems

        Chosen by Famous People

Edited by NIALL MACMONAGLE

With a Foreword by SEAMUS HEANEY

Compiled by:
Joann Bradish
Jacki Erskine
Carolyn Gibson
Steven Given
Julie Grantham
Paula Griffin
Nicola Hughes
Jonathan Logue
Collette Lucy
Duncan Lyster
Alice McEleney
Joy Marshall

PENGUIN BOOKS

PENGUIN BOOKS

Published by the Penguin Group
Penguin Books Ltd, 27 Wrights Lane, London w8 5tz, England
Penguin Books USA Inc., 375 Hudson Street, New York, New York 10014, USA
Penguin Books Australia Ltd, Ringwood, Victoria, Australia
Penguin Books Canada Ltd, 10 Alcorn Avenue, Toronto, Ontario, Canada m4v 3b2
Penguin Books (NZ) Ltd, 182–190 Wairau Road, Auckland 10, New Zealand

Penguin Books Ltd, Registered Offices: Harmondsworth, Middlesex, England

First published in individual volumes 1985, 1988, 1990 and 1992 by The Underground Press
Published as a collected edition titled *Lifelines: Letters from Famous People about Their Favourite
Poem*, edited by Niall MacMonagle and published by Town House and Country House with
Wesley College 1992
This selection, made by Penguin Books, published in 1993
10 9 8 7 6 5 4 3 2 1

This selection copyright © Town House and Country House with Wesley College, 1993
Letters copyright © individual contributors, 1985, 1988, 1990, 1992
Foreword copyright © Seamus Heaney, 1993
Preface copyright © Paula Griffin, Nicola Hughes and Alice McEleney, 1993
All rights reserved

The permissions on pp. 215–17 constitute an extension of this copyright page

Filmset in 10/12 pt Monophoto Bembo
Typeset by Datix International Limited, Bungay, Suffolk
Printed in England by Clays Ltd, St Ives plc

CONTENTS

For the children of the Third World

Children in famine . . . and the whole
world of loneliness, poverty, and pain
make a mockery of what human life
should be.

— Bertrand Russell

PREFACE

The *Lifelines* project was set in motion in the spring of 1985 when Steven Given, Collette Lucy and Joy Marshall, three Fifth Year students from this school, wanted to do something to help the people suffering from famine in Ethiopia. They wrote to famous people and asked them to name a favourite poem. The replies were compiled and *Lifelines* was born. The book, which was cheaply produced, was a sell-out and all profits were sent to help those in the developing world. In 1988 Julie Grantham, Jonathan Logue and Duncan Lyster compiled *Lifelines II*, and in 1990 Joann Bradish, Jacki Erskine and Carolyn Gibson compiled *Lifelines III*.

Earlier this year we published *Lifelines IV*. We are delighted that all four have been published in a collected edition by Town House and Country House and that selections appear in the present edition by Penguin.

We wrote to everyone that we (and our friends!) could think of and we are very grateful to those who replied. We would also like to thank Seamus Heaney for his kindness in writing the Foreword and Niall MacMonagle, our English teacher, who oversaw the project.

We hope that you enjoy the collection. There is a wonderful selection of poetry here: the higgledy-piggledy arrangement emphasizes the richness and the variety of the poems themselves. You are supporting a very good cause if you buy this book and perhaps your knowledge of poetry will be widened. Ours certainly was.

Paula Griffin
Nicola Hughes
Alice McEleney

Wesley College
Dublin

FOREWORD

Towards the end of Ford Madox Ford's sequence of First World War novels, *Parade's End*, there is a scene where the protagonist, Tietjens, is preparing the soldiers under his command to sustain a barrage from the German artillery. His mind is vividly alert to the trench activity and the shelling which surround him, but it is equally receptive to memories and associations swimming in, pell-mell, from other, remoter strata of his consciousness. He remembers, for example, a gunner telling him that it had probably cost the two armies a total of three million pounds sterling to reduce a twenty-acre field between the lines to a pulverized nowhere; and this memory has itself been prompted by an earlier, random image of 'the quiet thing', the heavy-leaved, timbered hedgerows around the parsonage at Bemerton, outside Salisbury, where the poet George Herbert had lived two centuries earlier. Inevitably, the sweetness and fortitude of Herbert's poetry come to mind then also, so that Tietjens's sense of value in the face of danger is both clarified and verified by the fleeting recollection of a couple of his favourite lines.

Jon Stallworthy directed my attention to this passage of Ford's after he had heard me refer to a similar moment in the life of George Seferis, when Seferis came to a realization (recorded in his *Journals*) that the work of his fellow Greek poet, Constantine Cavafy, was 'strong enough to help'. And it seems relevant to cite both occasions here again, in the foreword to a book which testifies in its own uninsistent fashion to the ways in which individuals still continue to recognize that some part of the meaning of their lives is lodged in the words and cadences of cherished passages of verse.

Meaning and value, of course, do not always entail a lofty note and an earnest message: it has been said, for example, that it would be worth a poet's while to spend a lifetime at work in order to leave behind one limerick that might distract somebody walking the last few yards to the electric chair. Certainly the pages that follow reveal that people of great talents and responsibilities do not repose their imaginative trust only in the sonorities of the Bible or the canonical voice of Shakespeare; they also turn to less solemn achievements, such as Lewis Carroll's nonsense verse, or the devastatingly light touch of Stevie Smith, or the merry logic of the early Irish 'The Monk and His Pet Cat' – chosen respectively by Amy Clampitt, Glenda Jackson and the late Cardinal Tomás Ó Fiaich.

Other choices were made because the contributor possessed a definite sense of the figure he or she must cut in the public eye: when Michael Holroyd selected 'Biography' by D. J. Enright, and Jeffrey Archer called for Kipling, and Sister Stanislaus picked 'Street Corner Christ', they did so in the knowledge that their poems would be read in the light of their known professions and commitments. And the same kind of compatibility operates in the case of critics like Helen Vendler and Christopher Ricks, whose choices of Stevens and Tennyson complement what we know about their literary preferences from other quarters. But when Conor Cruise O'Brien chose Milton's ode 'On the Morning of Christ's Nativity' and Chaim Herzog picked 'The Lake Isle of Innisfree', they were declaring obliquely that as private persons they live within a field of cultural force which may be at some odds with the general perception of them as public figures.

Writers, on the other hand, live precisely at the intersection of the public and the private, and it is interesting to see how their choices indulge or deflect our natural wish to establish connections between the style of what they write and what they read. Almost every selection by a poet here is corroborative of some aspect of his or her own published work, and there is a corresponding aptness to the choices made by many of the prose writers: that V. S. Pritchett should go for Clough, Jennifer Johnston for Holub, Ben Kiely for Robinson and John Banville for Celan, makes sense immediately, but there's surely just a little bit of decoy activity going on when the realistic Drabble goes for the prophetic Blake and the comedian Lodge promotes the tragedian Yeats.

This anthology was a magnificent idea from the start. The initial dedication of the pupils and their teacher at Wesley College (and, in particular, of the student compilers of *Lifelines*) was admirable; and the end result – itself only a selection from four packed, invigorating issues – is a book in which poems re-enter the world refreshed

rather than jaded by their long confinement inside people's heads, a
book that is surprisingly various and compulsively readable. It is,
after all, greatly heartening to discover that the poems of Keats and
Yeats are stored like imaginative fossil fuel in the minds of the
President of Harvard and the President of the State of Israel respect-
ively; and to be provided with such credible evidence that poetry
does indeed survive, as W. H. Auden said it would, 'a way of
happening, a mouth'.

Seamus Heaney

ACKNOWLEDGEMENTS:
A Note from the Editor and the Compilers

The *Lifelines* project was seven years in the making and we are very grateful to the following who helped bring it to completion: Christopher Adam, Philip Armitage, Kate Bateman, Kenneth Blackmore, Sarah Boles, Susan Brennan, Gillian Brownell, Eda Byrne, Frank Cinnamond, Caleb Clarke, Helen Clayton, Mary Clayton, Emma Coburn, Paul Coffey, Desmond Corbett, Susan Ellis, Craig Fox, Ewan Gibson, John Gillespie, Trevor Gillis, Richard Goodbody, Nicholas Graham, Gillian Hayden, Karen Henderson, Susan Henderson, Josephine Hughes, Peter Jennings, Carol Johnson, Mavis Johnson, Marybeth Joyce, Stanford Kingston, Stephen Kirk, Angela Logue, David Logue, Helen Lovell, Mervyn McCullagh, Ingrid McKenna, Rachel Macmanus, John MacMonagle, Sean MacMonagle, Craig McMurrough, Hazel Marshall, Linda Miller, Elizabeth O'Donnell, Michael O'Donnell, Cliona O'Dwyer, Christopher Pillow, Rachel Pope, Jeanne Prendergast, Rosemary Roe, Elizabeth Sibley, Thelma Smyth, Leigh Standing, Julie Sutton, Clare Thorp, Christopher Van Der Lee, Emma Walls and David Warren.

And a very special word of thanks to Treasa Coady, Elaine Campion and Bernie Daly of Town House and Country House.

Many contributors submitted their preferred editions of a text. Readers: Please note that if *your* version of a favourite poem varies from ours in spelling or punctuation, this is because a different edition may have been used.

TED HUGHES
Donal Og, Anonymous

My favourite poem is 'Donal Og' in Lady Gregory's translation. Why is this my favourite? I think no short poem has ever hit me so hard, or stayed with me so closely.

There's my reason why.

All my best to you.
TED HUGHES

Donal Og

It is late last night the dog was speaking of you;
the snipe was speaking of you in her deep marsh.
It is you are the lonely bird through the woods;
and that you may be without a mate until you find me.

You promised me, and you said a lie to me,
that you would be before me where the sheep are flocked;
I gave a whistle and three hundred cries to you,
and I found nothing there but a bleating lamb.

You promised me a thing that was hard for you,
a ship of gold under a silver mast;
twelve towns with a market in all of them,
and a fine white court by the side of the sea.

You promised me a thing that is not possible,
that you would give me gloves of the skin of a fish;
that you would give me shoes of the skin of a bird;
and a suit of the dearest silk in Ireland.

When I go by myself to the Well of Loneliness,
I sit down and I go through my trouble;
when I see the world and do not see my boy,
he that has an amber shade in his hair.

It was on that Sunday I gave my love to you;
the Sunday that is last before Easter Sunday.
And myself on my knees reading the Passion;
and my two eyes giving love to you for ever.

My mother said to me not to be talking with you today,
or tomorrow, or on the Sunday;
it was a bad time she took for telling me that;
it was shutting the door after the house was robbed.

My heart is as black as the blackness of the sloe,
or as the black coal that is on the smith's forge;
or as the sole of a shoe left in white halls;
it was you put that darkness over my life.

You have taken the east from me; you have taken the west
    from me;
you have taken what is before me and what is behind me;
you have taken the moon, you have taken the sun from
    me;
and my fear is great that you have taken God from me!

Anonymous
From the Irish
(Translated by Lady Augusta Gregory)

EAVAN BOLAND
Upon Julia's Clothes, Robert Herrick

This is written by Robert Herrick who died fourteen years after the
Restoration in 1660. He has come to be known as a Caroline poet but I
think the title is misleading. He is a late, upbeat and maverick Elizabethan.
This is certainly one of my favourite poems. For a piece supposedly written
by a court poet it practises remarkable thrift. I like the miserly economy of
language played off against the wonderful, prosperous image of the woman
in silks.

With best wishes for the project,
EAVAN BOLAND

Upon Julia's Clothes

Whenas in silks my Julia goes,
Then, then, methinks, how sweetly flows
That liquefaction of her clothes.

Next, when I cast mine eyes, and see
That brave vibration, each way free,
O, how that glittering taketh me!

Robert Herrick (1591–1674)

GARRET FITZGERALD
From *The Book of Ecclesiastes*

Dear Collette,

Many thanks for your letter. I must admit I find your plan to raise money for the Third World very original, as this is the first occasion on which I have been asked for my favourite poem.

I have, from time to time, come across a poem I have enjoyed reading, but quite frankly, on considering your letter, I found it difficult to pinpoint any one particular poem. However, I am particularly fond of the enclosed extract from The Book of Ecclesiastes, the words of which I find thought-provoking and profound, and like to reflect on in the rare moments when I can tear myself away from the hurly-burly of political life. I hope this will be of assistance to you.

Wishing you, Joy and Steven every success with the undertaking.

Yours sincerely,
GARRET FITZGERALD

From *The Book of Ecclesiastes*

All things have their season, and in their times all things
    pass under heaven.
A time to be born, and a time to die.
A time to plant, and a time to pluck up that which is
    planted.
A time to kill, and a time to heal.
A time to destroy, and a time to build.
A time to weep, and a time to laugh.
A time to mourn, and a time to dance.
A time to scatter stones, and a time to gather.
A time to embrace, and a time to be far from embraces.
A time to get, and a time to lose.
A time to keep, and a time to cast away.
A time to rend, and a time to sew.
A time to keep silence, and a time to speak.
A time of love, and a time of hatred.
A time of war, and a time of peace.
What hath man more of his labour?

ULICK O'CONNOR
Leda and the Swan, W. B. Yeats

Dear Students,

I have no favourite poem but I have a number of favourite poems. One is
'Leda and the Swan' by William Butler Yeats, whose last house in Ireland
was quite near you in Rathfarnham.

    The reason I like this poem is that it combines a magnificent gift for
poetic language with a very modern form. We see Leda, a beautiful girl

walking on the banks of a river when she is suddenly ambushed by the god Zeus, in the form of a swan. According to the belief of the ancient Greeks, this event resulted in the birth of Helen of Troy, which is the explanation of the lines:

> A shudder in the loins engenders there
> The broken wall, the burning roof and tower
> And Agamemnon dead.

You will, no doubt, know one of the causes of the Trojan War centred around Helen of Troy. It might interest you to know that this is a favourite poem of John Mortimer, QC, the well-known English playwright.

Yours sincerely,
ULICK O'CONNOR

Leda and the Swan

A sudden blow: the great wings beating still
Above the staggering girl, her thighs caressed
By the dark webs, her nape caught in his bill,
He holds her helpless breast upon his breast.

How can those terrified vague fingers push
The feathered glory from her loosening thighs?
And how can body, laid in that white rush,
But feel the strange heart beating where it lies?

A shudder in the loins engenders there
The broken wall, the burning roof and tower
And Agamemnon dead.
                          Being so caught up,
So mastered by the brute blood of the air,
Did she put on his knowledge with his power
Before the indifferent beak could let her drop?

W. B. Yeats
(1865–1939)

ANDREW MOTION
They Flee from Me, Thomas Wyatt

Dear Collette Lucy, Joy Marshall and Steven Given,
Thank you for your letter, and for inviting me to help you further your excellent idea.

'They Flee from Me', by Thomas Wyatt, is a poem I admire enormously. Although very well known, its long exposure to the public gaze has done nothing to dim the power of its eroticism, or to weaken the ways in which private feelings are related to public issues. And the marvellously adroit irregularities of its metre guarantee (among other things) that the freshness never fades from its conversational tone.

Good wishes,
ANDREW MOTION

They Flee from Me

They flee from me, that sometime did me seke
With naked fote stalkyng within my chamber,
Once have I seen them gentle, tame, and meke,
That now are wild, and do not once remember
That sometyme they have put them selves in danger,
To take bread at my hand, and now they range,
Busily sekyng in continuall change.

Thanked be fortune, it hath bene otherwise
Twenty tymes better: but once especiall,
In thinne aray, after a pleasant gyse,
When her loose gowne did from her shoulders fall,
And she me caught in her armes long and small,
And therwithall, so swetely did me kysse,
And softly sayd: deare hart, how like you this?

It was no dreame: for I lay broade awakyng.
But all is turnde now through my gentlenesse,
Into a bitter fashion of forsakyng:

And I have leave to go of her goodnesse,
And she also to use newfanglenesse.
But, sins that I unkyndly so am served:
How like you this, what hath she now deserved?

Thomas Wyatt
(1503–1542)

HUGH LEONARD
From *The Old Vicarage, Grantchester*, Rupert Brooke

Dear Anthologists,
My favourite poem is far too long to be included in an anthology, but I'll leave it to you to choose an excerpt. It is 'The Old Vicarage, Grantchester' by Rupert Brooke. It evokes, more than any other poem I know, a love of place – in this case rural England – and a longing for bygone summers. I can think of no richer imagery than

> Oh! there are chestnuts, summer through
> Beside the river made for you
> A tunnel of green gloom, and sleep
> Deeply above.

The poem becomes a litany of place names. Other villages are dismissed with rural slanders, when compared with the perfection of Grantchester, and finally there is that great couplet which embraces a mood, a way of life and a perpetual summer of french windows, lawns, fields and a solitary church tower:

> Stands the Church clock at ten to three?
> And is there honey still for tea?

Yours sincerely,
HUGH LEONARD

From *The Old Vicarage, Grantchester*

(Café des Westens, Berlin, May 1912)

God! I will pack, and take a train,
And get me to England once again!
For England's the one land I know,
Where men with Splendid Hearts may go;
And Cambridgeshire, of all England,
The shire for Men who Understand;
And of that district I prefer
The lovely hamlet Grantchester . . .

Ah God! to see the branches stir
Across the moon at Grantchester!
To smell the thrilling-sweet and rotten
Unforgettable, unforgotten
River-smell and hear the breeze
Sobbing in the little trees.
Say, do the elm-clumps greatly stand
Still guardians of that holy land?
The chestnut shade, in reverend dream,
The yet unacademic stream?
Is dawn a secret shy and cold
Anadyomene, silver-gold?
And sunset still a golden sea
From Haslingfield to Madingley?
And after, ere the night is born,
Do hares come out about the corn?
Oh, is the water sweet and cool,
Gentle and brown, above the pool?
And laughs the immortal river still
Under the mill, under the mill?
Say, is there Beauty yet to find?
And Certainty? and Quiet kind?
Deep meadows yet, for to forget
The lies, and truths, and pain? . . . Oh! yet
Stands the Church clock at ten to three?
And is there honey still for tea?

Rupert Brooke
(1887–1915)

BRENDAN KENNELLY
The Garden of Love, William Blake

Collette, Joy, Steven,
Thank you for writing to me. I think my favourite poem in the English language is 'The Garden of Love' by William Blake. I like it because it is a celebration of freedom.

Yours sincerely,
BRENDAN KENNELLY

The Garden of Love

I went to the Garden of Love,
And saw what I never had seen:
A Chapel was built in the midst,
Where I used to play on the green.

And the gates of this Chapel were shut
And Thou shalt not. writ over the door;
So I turn'd to the Garden of Love,
That so many sweet flowers bore,

And I saw it was filled with graves,
And tomb-stones where flowers should be:
And Priests in black gowns, were walking their rounds,
And binding with briars, my joys & desires.

William Blake
(1757–1827)

BERNARD MAC LAVERTY
The Introduction, Louis MacNeice

Dear Collette,
Thank you for your letter. I would be delighted to choose a poem for your anthology.

It has to be another Ulsterman.

The Introduction

They were introduced in a grave glade
And she frightened him because she was young
And thus too late. Crawly crawly
Went the twigs above their heads and beneath
The grass beneath their feet the larvae
Split themselves laughing. Crawly crawly
Went the cloud above the treetops reaching
For a sun that lacked the nerve to set
And he frightened her because he was old
And thus too early. Crawly crawly
Went the string quartet that was tuning up
In the back of the mind. You two should have met
Long since, he said, or else not now.
The string quartet in the back of the mind
Was all tuned up with nowhere to go.
They were introduced in a green grave.

Louis MacNeice
(1907–1963)

This is a favourite poem of mine, dealing as it does with missed opportunity and indecision. Above all there is the wit of MacNeice in the way he treats his subject and the total control he exerts over words. He can make the unexpected work.

Good luck with the whole enterprise.
BERNARD MAC LAVERTY

BENEDICT KIELY
Mr Flood's Party,
Edwin Arlington Robinson

Dear Collette, Joy and Steven,
Dylan Thomas said, 'Read poetry until you find what you like and then read it again. So that you may always have a few poems in your head even when you have no book before you.' So I always have a few favourite poems, changing, going away, going away, returning. I have a few at the moment but I send you this one by E.A.R.

Why do I like it? The poem speaks for itself. Padraic Colum, who was a good friend of mine, knew Arlington well in the States and spoke a lot about him. A strange man. Good luck with your project.

BEN KIELY

Mr Flood's Party

Old Eben Flood, climbing alone one night
Over the hill between the town below
And the forsaken upland hermitage
That held as much as he should ever know
On earth again of home, paused warily.
The road was his with not a native near;
And Eben, having leisure, said aloud,
For no man else in Tilbury to hear:

'Well, Mr Flood, we have the harvest moon
Again, and we may not have many more;
The bird is on the wing, the poet says,
And you and I have said it here before.
Drink to the bird.' He raised up to the light
The jug that he had gone so far to fill,
And answered huskily: 'Well, Mr Flood,
Since you propose it, I believe I will.'

Alone, as if enduring to the end
A valiant armor of scarred hopes outworn,
He stood there in the middle of the road
Like Roland's ghost winding a silent horn.
Below him, in the town among the trees,
Where friends of other days had honored him,
A phantom salutation of the dead
Rang thinly till old Eben's eyes were dim.

Then, as a mother lays her sleeping child
Down tenderly, fearing it may awake,
He set the jug down slowly at his feet
With trembling care, knowing that most things break;
And only when assured that on firm earth
It stood, as the uncertain lives of men
Assuredly did not, he paced away,
And with his hand extended paused again:

'Well, Mr Flood, we have not met like this
In a long time; and many a change has come
To both of us, I fear, since last it was
We had a drop together. Welcome home!'
Convivially returning with himself,
Again he raised his jug up to the light;
And with an acquiescent quaver said:
'Well, Mr Flood, if you insist, I might.

'Only a very little, Mr Flood –
For auld lang syne. No more, sir; that will do.'
So, for the time, apparently it did,
And Eben evidently thought so too;
For soon amid the silver loneliness
Of night he lifted up his voice and sang,
Secure, with only two moons listening,
Until the whole harmonious landscape rang –

'For auld lang syne.' The weary throat gave out,
The last word wavered; and the song was done,
He raised again the jug regretfully
And shook his head, and was again alone.

There was not much that was ahead of him,
And there was nothing in the town below –
Where strangers would have shut the many doors
That many friends had opened long ago.

Edwin Arlington Robinson
(1869–1935)

JOHN BANVILLE
Psalm, Paul Celan

Dear Collette Lucy, Joy Marshall, Steven Given:
There is no single poem which I would describe as my favourite. However, here is the text of a very beautiful poem, which I think would be particularly suitable for your anthology. It is by Paul Celan (1920–1970), a Jewish poet who wrote in German. As a child during World War II he was a prisoner in a Romanian labour camp. His parents were killed by the Nazis. Out of these terrible experiences he created a heartbreaking poetry.

Celan's poetry is very difficult to translate, so I hope you can carry the German as well as the English translation. Even though many readers will not know German, the look of the original is important.

I wish you the best of luck with your venture.

JOHN BANVILLE

Psalm

Niemand knetet uns wieder aus Erde und Lehm,
niemand bespricht unsern Staub.
Niemand.

Gelobt seist du, Niemand.
Dir zulieb wollen
wir blühn.
Dir
entgegen.

Ein Nichts
waren wir, sind wir, werden
wir bleiben, blühend:
die Nichts –, die
Niemandsrose.

Mit
dem Griffel seelenhell
dem Staubfaden himmelswüst,
der Krone rot
vom Purpurwort, das wir sangen
über, o über
dem Dorn.

Paul Celan
(1920–1970)

Psalm

No one moulds us again out of earth and clay,
no one conjures our dust.
No one.

Praised be your name, no one.
For your sake
we shall flower.
Towards
you.

A nothing
we were, are, shall
remain, flowering;
the nothing –, the
no one's rose.

With our pistil soul-bright
with our stamen heaven-ravaged
our corolla red
with the crimson word which we sang
over, o over
the thorn.

(Translated by Michael Hamburger)

IRIS MURDOCH
A Summer Night, W. H. Auden

This marvellously beautiful elegiac song, full of magisterial images, expresses both fear and hope. It also conjures up, with great tenderness and feeling, a particular occasion. This connection of vast moral vistas with individual situations is typical poetic magic.

IRIS MURDOCH

A Summer Night
(To Geoffrey Hoyland)

Out on the lawn I lie in bed,
Vega conspicuous overhead
  In the windless nights of June,
As congregated leaves complete
Their day's activity; my feet
  Point to the rising moon.

Lucky, this point in time and space
Is chosen as my working place,
  Where the sexy airs of summer,

The bathing hours and the bare arms,
The leisured drives through a land of farms
    Are good to a newcomer.

Equal with colleagues in a ring
I sit on each calm evening
    Enchanted as the flowers
The opening light draws out of hiding
With all its gradual dove-like pleading,
    Its logic and its powers:

That later we, though parted then,
May still recall these evenings when
    Fear gave his watch no look;
The lion griefs loped from the shade
And on our knees their muzzles laid,
    And Death put down his book.

Now north and south and east and west
Those I love lie down to rest;
    The moon looks on them all,
The healers and the brilliant talkers
The eccentrics and the silent walkers,
    The dumpy and the tall.

She climbs the European sky,
Churches and power-stations lie
    Alike among earth's fixtures:
Into the galleries she peers
And blankly as a butcher stares
    Upon the marvellous pictures.

To gravity attentive, she
Can notice nothing here, though we
    Whom hunger does not move,
From gardens where we feel secure
Look up and with a sigh endure
    The tyrannies of love:

And, gentle, do not care to know,
Where Poland draws her eastern bow,
    What violence is done,
Nor ask what doubtful act allows
Our freedom in this English house,
    Our picnics in the sun.

Soon, soon, through dykes of our content
The crumpling flood will force a rent
    And, taller than a tree,
Hold sudden death before our eyes
Whose river dreams long hid the size
    And vigours of the sea.

But when the waters make retreat
And through the black mud first the wheat
    In shy green stalks appears,
When stranded monsters gasping lie,
And sounds of riveting terrify
    Their whorled unsubtle ears,

May these delights we dread to lose,
This privacy need no excuse
    But to that strength belong,
As through a child's rash happy cries
The drowned parental voices rise
    In unlamenting song.

After discharges of alarm
All unpredicted let them calm
    The pulse of nervous nations,
Forgive the murderer in his glass,
Tough in their patience to surpass
    The tigress her swift motions.

W. H. Auden
(1907–1973)

THEODORA FITZGIBBON
Poem in October, Dylan Thomas

Dear Collette Lucy et al.,

I only just received your letter as I was away in England and only just home before setting off again next week. What an impossible thing you ask: my favourite poem! There is no such thing as far as I am concerned, I love so many and it would be very difficult to choose one.

However, having said that, I suppose I must perhaps put Dylan (Thomas) high on my list. One of his I am particularly fond of is 'Poem in October'.

This poem means quite a lot to me for I remember Dylan talking about it and reading some of the lines just before he finished it. I still hear that wonderfully sonorous voice filling our small sitting-room with the music of his magical words.

Also we both shared a late October birthday which we sometimes spent together so it has a particular meaning. I had met him a few years earlier and by the time this poem was written we were firm friends.

Best wishes and all success to your venture,

Sincerely,
THEODORA FITZGIBBON

Poem in October

It was my thirtieth year to heaven
Woke to my hearing from harbour and neighbour wood
And the mussel pooled and the heron
Priested shore
The morning beckon
With water praying and call of seagull and rook
And the knock of sailing boats on the net webbed wall
Myself to set foot
That second
In the still sleeping town and set forth.

My birthday began with the water –
Birds and the birds of the winged trees flying my name
Above the farms and the white horses

                    And I rose
                In the rainy autumn
        And walked abroad in a shower of all my days.
High tide and the heron dived when I took the road
                Over the border
                And the gates
        Of the town closed as the town awoke.

        A springful of larks in a rolling
Cloud and the roadside bushes brimming with whistling
        Blackbirds and the sun of October
                Summery
                On the hill's shoulder,
Here were fond climates and sweet singers suddenly
Come in the morning where I wandered and listened
                To the rain wringing
                Wind blow cold
        In the wood faraway under me.

        Pale rain over the dwindling harbour
And over the sea wet church the size of a snail
        With its horns through mist and the castle
                Brown as owls
                But all the gardens
Of spring and summer were blooming in the tall tales
Beyond the border and under the lark full cloud.
                There could I marvel
                My birthday
        Away but the weather turned around.

        It turned away from the blithe country
And down the other air and the blue altered sky
        Streamed again with a wonder of summer
                With apples
                Pears and red currants
And I saw in the turning so clearly a child's
Forgotten mornings when he walked with his mother
                Through the parables
                Of sun light
        And the legends of the green chapels

And the twice told fields of infancy
That his tears burned my cheeks and his heart moved in
    mine.
    These were the woods the river and sea
        Where a boy
      In the listening
Summertime of the dead whispered the truth of his joy
To the trees and the stones and the fish in the tide.
      And the mystery
        Sang alive
Still in the water and singingbirds.

And there could I marvel my birthday
Away but the weather turned around. And the true
 Joy of the long dead child sang burning
        In the sun.
      It was my thirtieth
Year to heaven stood there then in the summer noon
Though the town below lay leaved with October blood.
    O may my heart's truth
      Still be sung
On this high hill in a year's turning.

Dylan Thomas
(1914–1953)

MARGARET DRABBLE
Never Seek to Tell Thy Love,
William Blake

Dear Collette, Joy and Steven,
Impossible to choose *one* favourite but never mind, here is one of my
favourites – the three stanzas by Blake that begin:

> Never seek to tell thy love

I love this poem because it is sad – I have always liked sad poems best, I
think – and because it is mysterious and yet compact and because it catches
the difficulty and fragility of love. I don't really know what it means, but I
respond to it very strongly.

I hope this arrives in time and good luck with your anthology.

Yours sincerely,
MARGARET DRABBLE

Never Seek to Tell Thy Love

Never seek to tell thy love
Love that never told can be;
For the gentle wind does move
Silently, invisibly.

I told my love, I told my love
I told her all my heart,
Trembling, cold, in ghastly fears –
Ah, she doth depart.

Soon as she was gone from me
A traveller came by
Silently, invisibly –
O, was no deny.

William Blake
(1757–1827)

T. P. FLANAGAN
Bogland, Seamus Heaney

Thank you for your letter. One of my favourite poems is Seamus Heaney's 'Bogland' – from *Door into the Dark*. This is not simply because he dedicated the poem to me, which naturally pleased me very much, but because he and I had been together at the poem's beginnings. Seamus and I and our families had spent Hallowe'en together in McFaddens Hotel at Gortahork in County Donegal. And he came with me when I went out sketching in the car. It was a dry luminous autumn, and after the hot summer of that year the bogland was burnt the colour of marmalade. We all stood on the beach watching marvellous sunsets, and, in the twilight let off fireworks from the sand dunes to please our children. The poem is a celebration for me of a very happy and creative time in both our lives.

Good luck with your project,
T. P. FLANAGAN

Bogland

(For T. P. Flanagan)

We have no prairies
To slice a big sun at evening –
Everywhere the eye concedes to
Encroaching horizon,

Is wooed into the cyclops' eye
Of a tarn. Our unfenced country
Is bog that keeps crusting
Between the sights of the sun.

They've taken the skeleton
Of the Great Irish Elk
Out of the peat, set it up
An astounding crate full of air.

Butter sunk under
More than a hundred years
Was recovered salty and white.
The ground itself is kind, black butter

Melting and opening underfoot,
Missing its last definition
By millions of years.
They'll never dig coal here,

Only the waterlogged trunks
Of great firs, soft as pulp.
Our pioneers kept striking
Inwards and downwards,

Every layer they strip
Seems camped on before.
The bogholes might be Atlantic seepage.
The wet centre is bottomless.

Seamus Heaney
(b. 1939)

TOMÁS Ó FIAICH
The Monk and His Pet Cat,
Anonymous

Dear Collette, Joy and Steven,
Thank you for your letter inquiring about my favourite poem. I have
many favourite poems and the one I would mention to you is 'Pangur
Bán', where an old monk in his scriptorium philosophizes on the meaning

of life for himself and his pet cat Pangur Bán. Every time I read the poem I can see the two of them in my mind's eye as each goes about his work.

I wish you every success with your project and remain,

Yours sincerely,
† TOMÁS Ó FIAICH
Cardinal Archbishop of Armagh

The Monk and His Pet Cat

(A marginal poem on *Codex S Pauli*, by a student of the monastery of Carinthia)

I and my white Pangur
Each has his special art;
His mind is set on hunting mice
Mine on my special craft.

Better than fame I love to rest
With close study of my little book;
White Pangur does not envy me,
He loves to ply his childish art.

When we two are alone in our house
It is a tale without tedium;
Each of us has games never ending
Something to sharpen our wit upon.

At times by feats of valour
A mouse sticks in his net,
While in my net there drops
A loved law of obscure meaning.

His eye, this flashing full one,
He points against the fence wall
While against the fine edge of science
I point my clear but feeble eye.

He is joyous with swift jumping
When a mouse sticks in his sharp claw,
And I too am joyous when I have grasped
The elusive but well loved problem.

Though we thus play at all times
Neither hinders the other –
Each is happy with his own art,
Pursues it with delight.

He is master of the work
Which he does every day
While I am master of my work
Bringing to obscure laws clarity.

Anonymous (eighth or early ninth century)
(Version based on translations by Whitley Stokes,
John Strachan and Kuno Meyer)

CYRIL CUSACK
A Christmas Childhood,
Patrick Kavanagh
Felix Randal, Gerard Manley Hopkins
Confiteor, Cyril Cusack

Dear Collette, Joy and Steven,
Let me congratulate you on this very original and laudable effort of yours
to succour the poor people of the Third World. The effort deserves every
support.

26]   Now, another thing, it is not clear to me whether you wish to have a poem selected from my own two slender volumes of published poetry or rather a poem I favour from the work of major poets. I think probably the latter, but to choose my 'favourite poem' of the many that appeal to me obviously presents a difficulty.

However, I think my only plan is to suggest two poems which for me have a special appeal, one by Hopkins, the other by Kavanagh; and one from myself.

'A Christmas Childhood' by Patrick Kavanagh

and

'Felix Randal' by Gerard Manley Hopkins

My reasons for these preferences are almost impossible to articulate because they are scarcely rational, rather are they intuitive. I respond to them emotionally, perhaps because I am an actor.

However, I may say that I relate to 'A Christmas Childhood' because – *vide* the title – it is a pure evocation of the poet's childhood, of a child's intake of beauty in so many forms and images, and through the experiences and details of his country life and home in its beginnings, a perfect recall of true innocence, spiritually significant and sustaining into age. And, of course, it is tenderly, exquisitely rendered in the verse.

This poem I have spoken for audience on two occasions, once in the National Concert Hall and again on Irish television, and on each occasion I found myself or, rather should I say, lost myself in identification with the poet as a child.

With this, as with 'Felix Randal', let it be said that identification with the poet is the most desirable condition for the rendering of true poetry, allowing no intrusion of 'theatricality' or pretence, or even a priority of technical excellence. And what endears me to this particular poem of Hopkins is the passionate, near Christlike compassion for 'child, Felix, poor Felix Randal', the farrier. And, however difficult, I would say, as in my experience, that the emotion will carry the speaker, identifying with the poet, even through the delicate intricacies of the verse. 'Felix Randal', some years ago, I was privileged to commit to record and I treasure the compliment I had from a fellow Jesuit of the poet–priest: that in hearing the record it was as though for him, in some mysterious way, he were listening to Gerard Manley Hopkins himself.

For my own poem which I enclose let it suffice that, as an actor, my preference for this over other poems I have written rests in the title.

Yours sincerely,
CYRIL CUSACK

A Christmas Childhood

I

One side of the potato-pits was white with frost –
How wonderful that was, how wonderful!
And when we put our ears to the paling-post
The music that came out was magical.

The light between the ricks of hay and straw
Was a hole in Heaven's gable. An apple tree
With its December-glinting fruit we saw –
O you, Eve, were the world that tempted me

To eat the knowledge that grew in clay
And death the germ within it! Now and then
I can remember something of the gay
Garden that was childhood's. Again

The tracks of cattle to a drinking-place,
A green stone lying sideways in a ditch
Or any common sight the transfigured face
Of a beauty that the world did not touch.

II

My father played the melodeon
Outside at our gate;
There were stars in the morning east
And they danced to his music.

Across the wild bogs his melodeon called
To Lennons and Callans.
As I pulled on my trousers in a hurry
I knew some strange thing had happened.

Outside the cow-house my mother
Made the music of milking;
The light of her stable-lamp was a star
And the frost of Bethlehem made it twinkle.

A water-hen screeched in the bog,
Mass-going feet
Crunched the wafer-ice on the pot holes,
Somebody wistfully twisted the bellows wheel.

My child poet picked out the letters
On the grey stone,
In silver the wonder of a Christmas townland,
The winking glitter of a frosty dawn.

Cassiopeia was over
Cassidy's hanging hill,
I looked and three whin bushes rode across
The horizon – the Three Wise Kings.

An old man passing said:
'Can't he make it talk' –
The melodeon. I hid in the doorway
And tightened the belt of my box-pleated coat.

I nicked six nicks on the door-post
With my penknife's big blade –
There was a little one for cutting tobacco.
And I was six Christmases of age.

My father played the melodeon,
My mother milked the cows,
And I had a prayer like a white rose pinned
On the Virgin Mary's blouse.

                    Patrick Kavanagh
                    (1904–1967)

Felix Randal

Felix Randal the farrier, O he is dead then? my duty all
    ended,
Who have watched his mould of man, big-boned and
    hardy-handsome

Pining, pining, till time when reason rambled in it and
    some
Fatal four disorders, fleshed there, all contended?

Sickness broke him. Impatient, he cursed at first, but
    mended
Being anointed and all; though a heavenlier heart began
    some
Months earlier, since I had our sweet reprieve and ransom
Tendered to him. Ah well, God rest him all road ever he
    offended!

This seeing the sick endears them to us, us too it endears.
My tongue had taught thee comfort, touch had quenched
    thy tears,
Thy tears that touched my heart, child, Felix, poor Felix
    Randal;

How far from then forethought of, all thy more boisterous
    years,
When thou at the random grim forge, powerful amidst
    peers,
Didst fettle for the great grey drayhorse his bright and
    battering sandal!

Gerard Manley Hopkins
(1844–1889)

Confiteor

O dear my Lord, but what a tricky
cute and cunning customer in me
you have across your counter, one
eluding true communion's equity.

That you, you Three in One and One in Three,
could fail to see through me, could be
wide open to my wide-eyed bribery
or guiltily contrive –

you, Father, Holy Spirit and the Son –
to look the other way, conniving
at the filching and the fun
of taking all for free . . . say
which of us would thus betray,
pretending Satan's not alive!

O I can fake and I can fable,
I can fiddle, fib and fumble,
glibly gamble with you, Lord
(and tell me, boys, who better able!)
provide you do not grumble
that I blunt Saint Michael's sword,
lay not all my cards upon your table,
refusing me, accusing me
that I, I only ape humility,
in pride but feigning to be humble.

I myself with guiltless smile
myself beguiling, shall I you beguile!

Cyril Cusack
(b. 1910)

SEAMUS HEANEY
Cuchulain Comforted, W. B. Yeats

Dear Collette Lucy,
One of my favourite poems is 'Cuchulain Comforted' by W. B. Yeats.
Written a few days before his death, it is a mysterious and difficult poem,
but one which seems to fulfil Yeats's stated ambition 'to hold in a single
thought reality and justice'. It presents a confrontation between heroism
and cowardice, between violence and resignation, between life and death,
and communicates a deep sense of peace and understanding.

Sincerely,
SEAMUS HEANEY

Cuchulain Comforted

A man that had six mortal wounds, a man
Violent and famous, strode among the dead;
Eyes stared out of the branches and were gone.

Then certain Shrouds that muttered head to head
Came and were gone. He leant upon a tree
As though to meditate on wounds and blood.

A Shroud that seemed to have authority
Among those bird-like things came, and let fall
A bundle of linen. Shrouds by two and three

Came creeping up because the man was still.
And thereupon the linen-carrier said:
'Your life can grow much sweeter if you will

'Obey our ancient rule and make a shroud;
Mainly because of what we only know
The rattle of those arms makes us afraid.

'We thread the needles' eyes, and all we do
All must together do.' That done, the man
Took up the nearest and began to sew.

'Now we must sing and sing the best we can,
But first you must be told our character:
Convicted cowards all, by kindred slain

'Or driven from home and left to die in fear.'
They sang, but had nor human tunes nor words,
Though all was done in common as before;

They had changed their throats and had the throats of birds.

W. B. Yeats
(1865–1939)

FRANK MCGUINNESS
Sonnet 109, William Shakespeare

This is one of my favourite poems because it is an expression of great love and I wish someone had written it for me.

FRANK MCGUINNESS

Sonnet 109

O, never say that I was false of heart,
Though absence seemed my flame to qualify.
As easy might I from myself depart
As from my soul, which in thy breast doth lie.
That is my home of love; if I have ranged,
Like him that travels I return again,
Just to the time, not with the time exchanged,
So that myself bring water for my stain.
Never believe, though in my nature reigned
All frailties that besiege all kinds of blood,
That it could so preposterously be stained
To leave for nothing all thy sum of good;
   For nothing this wide universe I call
   Save thou, my rose; in it thou art my all.

William Shakespeare
(1564–1616)

GAY BYRNE
Jamie Jarr, Amanda Ros

Dear Compilers, all,

Glad to be included in your anthology. Hope you like my choice. I cannot say it's my *favourite* poem of all time, but I found my wife Kathleen reading it recently and it tickled my heart, for three reasons:

(1) I've been insulted, abused and kicked by TV viewers and radio listeners so often through the years, that I'm sadistically delighted when I see someone else getting a lash – even if they're dead.

(2) I'm a firm believer in the maxim that if you're going to do someone down, you should do a thorough job; and I think you'll agree that Amanda Ros does a thorough job on her hated lawyer. No pussyfooting or skirting the issue here – she lets her readers know precisely her opinion of the offending corpse.

(3) Anyone who has had a run-in with the legal profession in this country will relish the poem.

GAY BYRNE

Amanda Ros was born in County Down. Lived 1860–1939. She had a major grudge against people in the legal profession, for what reason I do not know.

Jamie Jarr

Here lies a blooming rascal
Once known as Jamie Jarr;
A lawyer of the lowest type,
Who loved your name to char.
Of clownish ways and manners,
He aped at speaking fine,
Which proved as awkward to him
As a drawing-room to swine.

I stood while the ground was hollowed
To admit this pile of stink;
They placed the coffin upside down
(The men upon the brink).
How the stony mould did thunder
Upon the coffin's rump,
The fainter grew the rattle
The deeper Jamie sunk.

His mouth now shut for ever,
His lying tongue now stark –
His 'paws' lie still, and never more
Can stab you in the dark.
Earth is by far the richer,
Hell – one boarder more –
Heaven rejoices to be free
From such a legal 'bore'.

Amanda Ros
(1860–1939)

MICHAEL HOLROYD
Biography, D. J. Enright

Dear Julie Grantham, Jonathan Logue and Duncan Lyster,
Thanks for your letter inviting me to choose a favourite poem and give a
reason for my choice.

'Biography' by D. J. Enright. I like this poem because it brings together
neatly and wittily, and with considerable feeling, the arguments against
what James Joyce called literary 'biografiends' such as myself. It's a humane
and appealing case that D. J. Enright pleads, and one that any biographer
should confront before deciding whether to write someone's Life. One
possible defence may be found in Pope's 'Essay on Man':

Know then thyself, presume not God to scan;
The proper study of mankind is man.

Good luck with the book which I hope makes a lot of money for Ethiopia.

Best wishes,
MICHAEL HOLROYD

Biography

Rest in one piece, old fellow
May no one make his money
Out of your odd poverty

Telling what you did
When the streets stared blankly back
And the ribbon fell slack

The girls you made
(And, worse, the ones you failed to)
The addled eggs you laid

Velleities that even you
Would hardly know you felt
But all biographers do

The hopes that only God could hear
(That great non-tattler)
Since no one else was near

What of your views on women's shoes?
If you collected orange peel
What *did* you do with the juice?

Much easier than your works
To sell your quirks
So burn your letters, hers and his –
Better no Life at all than this.

D. J. Enright
(b. 1920)

FLEUR ADCOCK
Holy Sonnets, X, John Donne

Dear Julie, Jonathan and Duncan,

Thank you for asking me to contribute to your book in aid of the Third World. Naturally I'm happy to do so, but I find it an extraordinarily difficult task. Because I'm involved with poetry all the time, I have hundreds of favourite poems, and I'm constantly adding new ones or changing my mind about old ones. I couldn't possibly settle for one. (Also some of them are far too long for your purpose.)

So what I'm sending you is a poem which has been one of my favourites for a long time: John Donne's sonnet, 'Death be not proud' (not a very original choice I'm afraid). Like many people's favourites, it's one that I've known by heart since I was at school: this means that I don't need to look it up when I want to be reminded of it; it's a permanent fixture in my mind. It's the kind of poem that would be comforting in circumstances of desperation or extremity, such as in prison or during a war – or so I imagine. It was included in the second book of poetry I ever bought (at sixteen; the first was by T. S. Eliot). I'm enclosing a copy of the text in the original spelling.

And good luck with the project!

Yours sincerely,
FLEUR ADCOCK

Holy Sonnets
X

Death be not proud, though some have called thee
Mighty and dreadfull, for, thou art not soe,
For, those, whom thou think'st, thou dost overthrow,
Die not, poore death, nor yet canst thou kill mee.
From rest and sleepe, which but thy pictures bee,
Much pleasure, then from thee, much more must flow,
And soonest our best men with thee doe goe,
Rest of their bones, and soules deliverie.
Thou art slave to Fate, Chance, kings, and desperate men,

And dost with poyson, warre, and sicknesse dwell,
And poppie, or charmes can make us sleepe as well,
And better then thy stroake; why swell'st thou then?
One short sleepe past, wee wake eternally,
And death shall be no more; death, thou shalt die.

John Donne
(1572–1631)

JOHN MONTAGUE
Sailing to Byzantium, W. B. Yeats

It is hard for me to choose *one* poem but if I had to, it would probably be 'Sailing to Byzantium'. I love its defiance, its clangour, and, while I have no desire to be a golden bird, I recognize and enjoy the final flourish, oratorical though it be!

JOHN MONTAGUE

Sailing to Byzantium

I

That is no country for old men. The young
In one another's arms, birds in the trees
– Those dying generations – at their song,
The salmon-falls, the mackerel-crowded seas,
Fish, flesh, or fowl, commend all summer long
Whatever is begotten, born, and dies.
Caught in that sensual music all neglect
Monuments of unageing intellect.

II

An aged man is but a paltry thing,
A tattered coat upon a stick, unless
Soul clap its hands and sing, and louder sing
For every tatter in its mortal dress,
Nor is there singing school but studying
Monuments of its own magnificence;
And therefore I have sailed the seas and come
To the holy city of Byzantium.

III

O sages standing in God's holy fire
As in the gold mosaic of a wall,
Come from the holy fire, perne in a gyre,
And be the singing-masters of my soul.
Consume my heart away; sick with desire
And fastened to a dying animal
It knows not what it is; and gather me
Into the artifice of eternity.

IV

Once out of nature I shall never take
My bodily form from any natural thing,
But such a form as Grecian goldsmiths make
Of hammered gold and gold enamelling
To keep a drowsy Emperor awake;
Or set upon a golden bough to sing
To lords and ladies of Byzantium
Of what is past, or passing, or to come.

W. B. Yeats
(1865–1939)

LAURIE LEE
Stopping by Woods on a Snowy Evening, Robert Frost

Dear Julie, Jonathan, Duncan,
'Stopping by Woods on a Snowy Evening' (Robert Frost).
   For its atmosphere and rhyme-scheme, timelessly satisfying.
   For its gauche imperfections –

> Whose woods these are I think I know.
> His house is in the village though

Well, does he or doesn't he?
And for the shattering repetition of the two last lines. A stumbling accident of writing, according to Frost, as most revelations are.

LAURIE LEE

Stopping by Woods on a Snowy Evening

Whose woods these are I think I know.
His house is in the village though;
He will not see me stopping here
To watch his woods fill up with snow.

My little horse must think it queer
To stop without a farmhouse near
Between the woods and frozen lake
The darkest evening of the year.

He gives his harness bells a shake
To ask if there is some mistake.
The only other sound's the sweep
Of easy wind and downy flake.

The woods are lovely, dark, and deep,
But I have promises to keep,
And miles to go before I sleep,
And miles to go before I sleep.

Robert Frost
(1874–1963)

PAUL DURCAN
Shut Up, I'm Going to Sing You a Love Song, Ellen Gilchrist

Dear Julie, Jonathan and Duncan,
I love good anthologies and *Lifelines I* was unquestionably one of the best anthologies put together anywhere in recent years. I am looking forward immensely, therefore, to *Lifelines II*.

I have hundreds of 'favourite poems'. Here are some titles as they come to mind: 'To my Wife' by Knut Hamsun; 'Innocent When You Dream' by Tom Waits; 'One Art' by Elizabeth Bishop; 'In St Etheldreda's' by Sara Berkeley; 'Almost Communication' by Rita Ann Higgins; 'The Dark Sobrietee' by Macdara Woods; 'White Shirts in Childhood' by Dermot Bolger; 'Summertime in England' by Van Morrison; 'To Margot Heinemann' by John Cornford; 'The Fall of Rome' by W. H. Auden; 'The Pleasant Joys of Brotherhood' by James Simmons; 'Sunday Morning' by Wallace Stevens; 'The Keen Stars were Twinkling' by Percy Shelley; 'In Parenthesis' by David Jones; 'Voracities and Verities Sometimes are Interacting' by Marianne Moore; 'Lisdoonvarna' by Christy Moore; 'The Bronze Horseman' by Alexander Pushkin; 'On Raglan Road' by Patrick Kavanagh; 'Four Quartets' by T. S. Eliot; 'Everness' by Jorge Luis Borges; 'One Too Many Mornings' by Bob Dylan; 'The Collar-Bone of a Hare' by W. B. Yeats; 'The Silken Tent' by Robert Frost; 'Thirty Bob a Week' by John Davidson; 'Of the Great and Famous Ever-to-be-honoured Knight, Sir Francis Drake, and of My Little-Little Self' by Robert Hayman; 'Return Thoughts' by Anthony Cronin; '7 Middagh Street' by Paul Muldoon; 'Ireland 1944' by Francis Stuart; 'Born in the USA' by Bruce Springsteen;

'Lament for Ignacio Sanchez Mejias' by Federico Garcia Lorca; 'Midnight
Trolleybus' by Bulat Okudjhava; 'Let's Be Sad' by Irina Ratushinskaya;
'He Among Them Nightly Moving' by John Stephen Moriarty; 'A Bat on
the Road' by Seamus Heaney; 'Barbara' by Jacques Prévert; 'Antarctica' by
Derek Mahon; 'Intoxication' by Boris Pasternak; 'Skrymtymnym' by
Andrei Voznesensky; 'The Princess of Parallelograms' by Medbh McGuckian;
'In the Luxembourg Gardens' by Tom McCarthy . . .

But the poem I would like you to play for me today is 'Shut Up, I'm
Going to Sing You a Love Song' by Ellen Gilchrist, an American word-
magician who is the author of at least two stunning books of stories, *Victory
Over Japan* and *In the Land of Dreamy Dreams*. I hope you collect buckets of
money for the people of Ethiopia.

Salut,
PAUL DURCAN

Shut Up, I'm Going to Sing You a Love Song

(For F. S. K.)

I dream to save you
I must leap from an ocean pier
into water of uncertain depth
You flail below me in a business suit
Knowing I must jump I frown
Knowing we will drown together
Knowing the dark sea will bloom for a moment
with the red hibiscus I refuse to wear
over either ear

Sighing I dive my special Red Cross dive
straight into the sea
which is deeper than either of us dreamed
it would be
Sit still there is nothing to fear
Undo my dress I am here you are here

Ellen Gilchrist
(b. 1935)

JENNIFER JOHNSTON
Fairy Tale, Miroslav Holub

Dear Three,
Thank you for your letter.

I can't possibly let you have the text of my FAVOURITE poem, as I have quite a few ... and anyway I expect that lots of people will send you the same poems over and over again. Here, however, is a short poem that I like very much and it seems to have relevance to what you are trying to do.

It is called 'Fairy Tale'.

It is written by a Czech poet called Miroslav Holub.

I don't know how you pronounce that, but that doesn't matter. It is simple, truthful and sad and filled with beautiful imagination.

It has for me the innocence and simplicity of a child's painting, bright, honest, unselfconscious, and the sad wisdom of the adult; all wrapped up into such a few lines.

I hope you like it also.

Good luck with the project and have a happy 1988.

Yours in friendship,
JENNIFER JOHNSTON

Fairy Tale

He built himself a house,
    his foundations,
    his stones,
    his walls,
    his roof overhead,
    his chimney and smoke,
    his view from the window.

He made himself a garden,
    his fence,
    his thyme,
    his earthworm,
    his evening dew.

He cut out his bit of sky above.

And he wrapped the garden in the sky
and the house in the garden
and packed the lot in a handkerchief
and went off
lone as an arctic fox
through the cold
unending
rain
into the world.

Miroslav Holub
(b. 1923)
(Translated by George Theiner)

DEREK MAHON
The Moose, Elizabeth Bishop

Dear Miss Grantham and friends,
I don't know if it's necessarily my favourite poem, but it's one I like very much: 'The Moose' by Elizabeth Bishop. The title is a pun on 'The Muse', and the poem describes a bus journey at night from Nova Scotia to Boston during which a moose appears on the road, to everyone's delighted astonishment. It's a poem about the magical in the ordinary, a poem about poetry itself in a sense: one of the great underrated poems of the century. I recommend it to all those who want to know what poetry means, and wish you well in your efforts on behalf of the Third World.

Sincerely,
DEREK MAHON

The Moose

(For Grace Bulmer Bowers)

From narrow provinces
of fish and bread and tea,
home of the long tides
where the bay leaves the sea
twice a day and takes
the herrings long rides,

where if the river
enters or retreats
in a wall of brown foam
depends on if it meets
the bay coming in,
the bay not at home;

where, silted red,
sometimes the sun sets
facing a red sea,
and others, veins the flats'
lavender, rich mud
in burning rivulets;

on red, gravelly roads,
down rows of sugar maples,
past clapboard farmhouses
and neat, clapboard churches,
bleached, ridged as clamshells,
past twin silver birches,

through late afternoon
a bus journeys west,
the windshield flashing pink,
pink glancing off of metal,
brushing the dented flank
of blue, beat-up enamel;

down hollows, up rises,
and waits, patient, while
a lone traveller gives
kisses and embraces
to seven relatives
and a collie supervises.

Goodbye to the elms,
To the farm, to the dog.
The bus starts. The light
grows richer; the fog,
shifting, salty, thin,
comes closing in.

Its cold, round crystals
form and slide and settle
in the white hens' feathers,
in gray glazed cabbages,
on the cabbage roses
and lupins like apostles;

the sweet peas cling
to their wet white string
on the whitewashed fences;
bumblebees creep
inside the foxgloves,
and evening commences.

One stop at Bass River.
Then the Economies –
Lower, Middle, Upper;
Five Islands, Five Houses,
where a woman shakes a tablecloth
out after supper.

A pale flickering. Gone.
The Tantramar marshes
and the smell of salt hay.
An iron bridge trembles
and a loose plank rattles
but doesn't give way.

On the left, a red light
swims through the dark:
a ship's port lantern.
Two rubber boots show,
illuminated, solemn.
A dog gives one bark.

A woman climbs in
with two market bags,
brisk, freckled, elderly.
'A grand night. Yes, sir,
all the way to Boston.'
She regards us amicably.

Moonlight as we enter
the New Brunswick woods,
hairy, scratchy, splintery;
moonlight and mist
caught in them like lamb's wool
on bushes in a pasture.

The passengers lie back.
Snores. Some long sighs.
A dreamy divagation
begins in the night,
a gentle, auditory,
slow hallucination . . .

In the creakings and noises,
an old conversation
— not concerning us,
but recognizable, somewhere,
back in the bus:
Grandparents' voices

uninterruptedly
talking, in Eternity:
names being mentioned,
things cleared up finally;
what he said, what she said,
who got pensioned;

deaths, deaths and sicknesses;
the year he remarried;
the year (something) happened.
She died in childbirth.
That was the son lost
when the schooner foundered.

He took to drink. Yes.
She went to the bad.
When Amos began to pray
even in the store and
finally the family had
to put him away.

'Yes . . .' that peculiar
affirmative. 'Yes . . .'
A sharp, indrawn breath,
half groan, half acceptance,
that means 'Life's like that.
We know *it* (also death).'

Talking the way they talked
in the old featherbed,
peacefully, on and on,
dim lamplight in the hall,
down in the kitchen, the dog
tucked in her shawl.

Now, it's all right now
even to fall asleep
just as on all those nights.
— Suddenly the bus driver
stops with a jolt,
turns off his lights.

A moose has come out of
the impenetrable wood
and stands there, looms, rather,
in the middle of the road.
It approaches; it sniffs at
the bus's hot hood.

Towering, antlerless,
high as a church,
homely as a house
(or, safe as houses).
A man's voice assures us
'Perfectly harmless . . .'

Some of the passengers
exclaim in whispers,
childishly, softly,
'Sure are big creatures.'
'It's awful plain.'
'Look! It's a she!'

Taking her time,
she looks the bus over,
grand, otherworldly.
Why, why do we feel
(we all feel) this sweet
sensation of joy?

'Curious creatures,'
says our quiet driver,
rolling his r's.
'Look at that, would you.'
Then he shifts gears.
For a moment longer,

by craning backward,
the moose can be seen
on the moonlit macadam;
then there's a dim
smell of moose, an acrid
smell of gasoline.

Elizabeth Bishop
(1911–1979)

MARY LELAND
An Arundel Tomb, Philip Larkin

Dear Editors,

Forgive my delay in replying to your request for a favourite poem; it was harder than I had expected to select just one. It seems that the proposed title of your collection – *Lifelines* – explains some part of the difficulty: poetry, and some prose, has provided me, as others, with lifelines when the going got rough – or even when some other way of describing something good or beautiful was required. And in either of those circumstances we need more than one lifeline to help us cling to what is important, real, and right.

My commonplace book has Pound, Vaughan, Arnold, and Housman, Mahon and Montague among others. Yeats and Kavanagh and Richard Murphy join Heaney, Kinsella, Jennings, and Heath-Stubbs on my shelves. At different times, in different ways, some of the work of all of these and of so many others has mattered, has helped or has inspired. It would not do, perhaps, for a desert island, but of them all I find myself still being grateful – thanks with admiration – for Philip Larkin's 'An Arundel Tomb'.

The last line answers an old question; the right answer, I want to think. As for the rest, I'm happy to know that when I stand, as I do at any opportunity, before the kind of effigies depicted in the poem and ponder at them, and at the people they enshrine, I am simply one of a whole community of observant wonderers.

Yours,
MARY LELAND

An Arundel Tomb

Side by side, their faces blurred,
The earl and countess lie in stone,
Their proper habits vaguely shown
As jointed armour, stiffened pleat,
And that faint hint of the absurd –
The little dogs under their feet.

Such plainness of the pre-baroque
Hardly involves the eye, until
It meets his left-hand gauntlet, still
Clasped empty in the other; and
One sees, with a sharp tender shock,
His hand withdrawn, holding her hand.

They would not think to lie so long.
Such faithfulness in effigy
Was just a detail friends would see:
A sculptor's sweet commissioned grace
Thrown off in helping to prolong
The Latin names around the base.

They would not guess how early in
Their supine stationary voyage
The air would change to soundless damage,
Turn the old tenantry away;
How soon succeeding eyes begin
To look, not read. Rigidly they

Persisted, linked, through lengths and breadths
Of time. Snow fell, undated. Light
Each summer thronged the glass. A bright
Litter of birdcalls strewed the same
Bone-riddled ground. And up the paths
The endless altered people came,

Washing at their identity.
Now, helpless in the hollow of
An unarmorial age, a trough
Of smoke in slow suspended skeins
Above their scrap of history,
Only an attitude remains:

Time has transfigured them into
Untruth. The stone fidelity
They hardly meant has come to be
Their final blazon, and to prove
Our almost-instinct almost true:
What will survive of us is love.

Philip Larkin
(1922–1985)

FINTAN O'TOOLE
I'm Explaining a Few Things,
Pablo Neruda

Dear Julie, Jonathan and Duncan,

Thanks very much for your letter and for the invitation to contribute to the book. My sincere congratulations on your initiative and dedication in producing a book – I have some idea of the amount of perseverance and sheer hard labour involved. It is terrible that such efforts should have any place in a supposedly civilized world, that other people's lives should depend on them. But so long as they do we are all prisoners of conscience.

I hope you like the poem I've chosen. It's by the Chilean Nobel Prize winner Pablo Neruda, who died of a heart-attack during the savage coup in his country in 1973. I've chosen it both because I think it's a wonderful poem and because I think it's appropriate to the inspiration of your book: our responsibility not to ignore the suffering of our fellow human beings. This is what I'd like to say about it:

Pablo Neruda's poem is both a work of great formal beauty and a statement of the insufficiency of beauty in an ugly world. Neruda, a poet of the magical and the mysterious, was Chile's consul in Madrid at the time of the Spanish Civil War. There, through the friendship of fellow-poets like Federico Garcia Lorca (the 'Federico' of the poem), murdered by the Fascists, he discovered his responsibility to his fellow man in the face of barbarity and atrocity. What is wonderful about the poem, however, is that the devastation of death is set against the vigour, colour and flow of life. The poem is tragic but also an affirmation of the joy of living. Against the accusation that he no longer writes 'pure poetry', Neruda puts forward both a vision of the richness of humanity and an invocation of the terror of its destruction by the Fascist bombing of Madrid. I can never read it without a mixture of horror, anger and hope.

Good luck with the entire project,

All the best,
FINTAN O'TOOLE

I'm Explaining a Few Things

You are going to ask: and where are the lilacs?
and the poppy-petalled metaphysics?
and the rain repeatedly spattering
its words and drilling them full
of apertures and birds?

I'll tell you all the news.

I lived in a suburb,
a suburb of Madrid, with bells,
and clocks, and trees.

From there you could look out
over Castile's dry face:
a leather ocean.

My house was called
the house of flowers, because in every cranny
geraniums burst: it was
a good-looking house
with its dogs and children.

Remember, Raul?
Eh, Rafael?
Federico, do you remember
From under the ground
my balconies on which
the light of June drowned flowers in your mouth?
Brother, my brother!

Everything
loud with big voices, the salt of merchandises,
pile-ups of palpitating bread,
the stalls of my suburb of Arguelles with its statue
like a drained inkwell in a swirl of hake:
oil flowed into spoons,
a deep baying
of feet and hands swelled in the streets,
metres, litres, the sharp
measure of life,
    stacked-up fish,
the texture of roofs with a cold sun in which
the weather vane falters,
the fine, frenzied ivory of potatoes,
wave on wave of tomatoes rolling down to the sea.

And one morning all that was burning,
one morning the bonfires
leapt out of the earth
devouring human beings –
and from then on fire,
gunpowder from then on,
and from then on blood.
Bandits with planes and moors
bandits with finger-rings and duchesses,
bandits with black friars spattering blessings
came through the sky to kill children
and the blood of children ran through the streets
without fuss, like children's blood.

Jackals that the jackals would despise,
stones that the dry thistle would bite on and spit out,
vipers that the vipers would abominate!

Face to face with you I have seen the blood
of Spain tower like a tide
to drown you in one wave
of pride and knives!

Treacherous
generals:
see my dead house,
look at broken Spain:
from every house burning metal flows
instead of flowers,
from every socket of Spain
Spain emerges
and from every dead child a rifle with eyes,
and from every crime bullets are born
which one day will find
the bull's eye of your hearts.

And you will ask: why doesn't his poetry
speak of dreams and leaves
and the great volcanoes of his native land?

Come and see the blood in the streets.
Come and see
the blood in the streets.
Come and see the blood
in the streets!

Pablo Neruda
(1904–1973)
(Translated by Nathaniel Tarn)

JEFFREY ARCHER
The Thousandth Man, Rudyard Ki...

Dear Miss Grantham,
Many thanks for your letter.

My favourite poem is 'The Thousandth Man' by Rudyard Kipling because it reflects my own attitude to loyalty and friendship. I am a great admirer of Kipling because he had a great command of the language as well as being a first-class story teller.

May I wish your project every success,

Yours sincerely,
JEFFREY ARCHER

The Thousandth Man

One man in a thousand, Solomon says,
Will stick more close than a brother.
And it's worth while seeking him half your days
If you find him before the other.
Nine hundred and ninety-nine depend
On what the world sees in you,
But the Thousandth Man will stand your friend
With the whole round world agin you.

'Tis neither promise nor prayer nor show
Will settle the finding for 'ee.
Nine hundred and ninety-nine of 'em go
By your looks, or your acts, or your glory.
But if he finds you and you find him,
The rest of the world don't matter;
For the Thousandth Man will sink or swim
With you in any water.

You can use his purse with no more talk
Than he uses yours for his spendings,
And laugh and meet in your daily walk
As though there had been no lendings.
Nine hundred and ninety-nine of 'em call
For silver and gold in their dealings;
But the Thousandth Man he's worth 'em all,
Because you can show him your feelings.

His wrong's your wrong, and his right's your right
In season or out of season.
Stand up and back it in all men's sight –
With *that* for your only reason!
Nine hundred and ninety-nine can't bide
The shame or mocking or laughter,
But the Thousandth Man will stand by your side
To the gallows-foot – and after!

Rudyard Kipling
(1865–1936)

MAEVE BINCHY
Back in the Playground Blues,
Adrian Mitchell

Dear Julie, Jonathan, Duncan,
I know Adrian Mitchell and have heard him reading his poetry from time
to time, but even though he has written poems which may have stronger
messages, poetry against war of all kinds, nothing ever struck me as being
so immediate and something that everyone could understand as this. We
have all been in a playground of some sort or other, there has always been
violence and hurt and cruelty. I saw this as a child and as a teacher. People
pick on others often without any idea of the damage and the hurt they have
caused.

But the end of the poem is very true and very full of hope. When you are older and more or less grown up it becomes easier to take charge of your own life and not to feel a victim of the bullies and those who wound you with words or with war in the Killing Ground.

All the best,
MAEVE BINCHY

Back in the Playground Blues

I dreamed I was back in the playground, I was
  about four feet high
Yes dreamed I was back in the playground,
  standing about four feet high
Well the playground was three miles long and
  the playground was five miles wide

It was broken black tarmac with a high wire
  fence all around
Broken black dusty tarmac with a high fence
  running all around
And it had a special name to it, they called
  it The Killing Ground

Got a mother and a father, they're one
  thousand years away
The rulers of The Killing Ground are coming
  out to play
Everybody thinking: 'Who they going to play
  with today?'

  Well you get it for being Jewish
  And you get it for being black
  Get it for being chicken
  And you get it for fighting back
  You get it for being big and fat
  Get it for being small
  Oh those who get it get it and get it
  For any damn thing at all

Sometimes they take a beetle, tear off its
    six legs one by one
Beetle on its black back, rocking in the
    lunchtime sun
But a beetle can't beg for mercy, a beetle's
    not half the fun

I heard a deep voice talking, it had that
    iceberg sound,
'It prepares them for Life' – but I have
    never found
Any place in my life worse than The Killing Ground.

Adrian Mitchell
(b. 1932)

JOHN GIELGUD
From *A Shropshire Lad*,
A. E. Housman

My favourite poem is 'Bredon Hill' from A. E. Housman's *Shropshire Lad*, as I spoke it for my first audition in 1921 when I got a scholarship at my first Dramatic School, and used to recite it at Troop Concerts during the war, and once very successfully in a Television Talk Show in America not many years ago.

Sincerely yours,
JOHN GIELGUD

XXI
Bredon Hill

In summertime on Bredon
  The bells they sound so clear;
Round both the shires they ring them
  In steeples far and near,
  A happy noise to hear.

Here of a Sunday morning
  My love and I would lie,
And see the coloured counties,
  And hear the larks so high
  About us in the sky.

The bells would ring to call her
  In valleys miles away:
'Come all to church, good people;
  Good people, come and pray.'
  But here my love would stay.

And I would turn and answer
  Among the springing thyme,
'Oh, peal upon our wedding,
  And we will hear the chime,
  And come to church in time.'

But when the snows at Christmas
  On Bredon top were strown,
My love rose up so early
  And stole out unbeknown
  And went to church alone.

They tolled the one bell only,
  Groom there was none to see,
The mourners followed after,
  And so to church went she,
  And would not wait for me.

The bells they sound on Bredon,
    And still the steeples hum,
'Come all to church, good people' –
    Oh, noisy bells, be dumb;
    I hear you, I will come.

A. E. Housman
(1859–1936)

T. A. FINLAY
The Death and Last Confession of Wandering Peter, Hilaire Belloc

Dear Julie Grantham, Jonathan Logue and Duncan Lyster,
Thank you very much for your letter concerning your project to produce a book called *Lifelines* for the purpose of raising funds for the Third World.

It is an excellent idea and I hope you are very successful with it.

It gives me great pleasure to take part in it and to give any assistance I can.

The poem which I have chosen is one of which I have been very fond for a long time: 'The Death and Last Confession of Wandering Peter', written by Hilaire Belloc.

The reason I have chosen this poem is that, firstly, I find it very felicitously expressed and beautifully written. Secondly, and more importantly, I have always been immensely attracted by the concept that Peter Wanderwide would, by reason of all the people he had known, of all the places he had seen and, I rather assume, of all the good company he had met with, find himself protected against too harsh a judgement on the Day of Judgement.

Furthermore, it seems to me that he retained up to the end of his life
what I consider to be one of the most precious of all attributes, and that
was a sense of humour. The concept of telling the 'Blessed doubtful things
of Val d'Aran and Perigord' seems always to me to be irresistible.

I wish you every success with your good project.

Yours sincerely,
T. A. FINLAY
An Príomh-Bhreitheamh
(Mr Justice Thomas A. Finlay, The Chief Justice)

The Death and Last Confession of Wandering Peter

When Peter Wanderwide was young
He wandered everywhere he would:
And all that he approved was sung,
And most of what he saw was good.

When Peter Wanderwide was thrown
By Death himself beyond Auxerre,
He chanted in heroic tone
To priests and people gathered there:

'If all that I have loved and seen
Be with me on the Judgment Day,
I shall be saved the crowd between
From Satan and his foul array.

'Almighty God will surely cry,
"St Michael! Who is this that stands
With Ireland in his dubious eye,
And Perigord between his hands,

'"And on his arm the stirrup-thongs,
And in his gait the narrow seas,
And in his mouth Burgundian songs,
But in his heart the Pyrenees?"

'St Michael then will answer right
(And not without angelic shame),
"I seem to know his face by sight:
I cannot recollect his name . . . ?"

'St Peter will befriend me then,
Because my name is Peter too:
"I know him for the best of men
That ever walloped barley brew.

'"And though I did not know him well
And though his soul were clogged with sin,
I hold the keys of Heaven and Hell.
Be welcome, noble Peterkin."

'Then shall I spread my native wings
And tread secure the heavenly floor,
And tell the Blessed doubtful things
Of Val d'Aran and Perigord.'

This was the last and solemn jest
Of weary Peter Wanderwide.
He spoke it with a failing zest,
And having spoken it, he died.

Hilaire Belloc
(1870–1953)

EILÉAN NÍ
CHUILLEANEÁIN
Houserules, Macdara Woods

Dear Julie, Jonathan, Duncan,
Thank you very much for your letter. I assume that when you ask for 'a favourite poem', you mean one by someone else, not my favourite among my own poems. I am enclosing a copy of a poem, 'Houserules', by Macdara Woods. I like it because it is about me – perhaps that's not a good reason. I like it as well, and more seriously, because it is about marriage in the modern world, it's both witty and a bit frightening. A reviewer called it 'horrific but adoring'. I think 'adoring' is too strong, the poem is too astringent for that.
   I hope both the poem and my reasons for liking it appeal to you.
   Good luck with your book.

Yours sincerely,
EILÉAN NÍ CHUILLEANEÁIN

Houserules

Hoop-la said my working wife
this woman says there were two sorts of amazons
(and she looked at me over her tee ell ess)
the ones that went in for househusbands
and the others . . . random copulators
who only hit the ground in spots

Measuring-up to my responsibilities
I called to my wife starting out for work
could you take my head in to town today please
have my hair cut and my beard trimmed
for this poetry-reading on Thursday
(I was dusting my high-heeled Spanish boots)

Gladly: she threw the talking head
in the back of the car with her lecture notes
her handbag fur coat and galley proofs
tricks of trade and mercantile accoutrements
Otrivine stuffed firmly up my nostrils
to stop catarrh and Hacks for my throat

Leaving me headless and in some straits:
considering the ways of well set-up amazons
as I fumbled helplessly around the garden
playing blind man's buff to a dancing clothesline
stubbing my pegs on air and thinking with envy
of my neighbour and his empire of cabbages.

Macdara Woods
(b. 1942)

KEVIN MYERS
The Gods of the Copybook Headings, Rudyard Kipling

I was brought up to believe that poetry should have rhyme, rhythm and resonance. One could declaim it. Good stuff with metres that would run on the lines of de-dum, de-dum, de-dum, de-da, de-dum, de-dum, de-dum, de-do . . . If you can't recite it t'ain't poetry.

As for my own choice, it is the stuff to give the troops when you're three sheets to the wind and about to pass out. Longfellow now, is the sort of fellow I'm talking about. Good manly stuff with punctuation and rhymes and pace you can beat time to.

And it is Kipling that I choose for my contribution – 'The Gods of the Copybook Headings' having just about everything. All the rhyme and the rhythm and the internal resonance that you could want. Plus a message. Good poems should always have a message.

KEVIN MYERS

The Gods of the Copybook Headings

As I pass through my incarnations in every age and race,
I make my proper prostrations to the Gods of the Market-
Place.
Peering through reverent fingers I watch them flourish
and fall,
And the Gods of the Copybook Headings, I notice, outlast
them all.

We were living in trees when they met us. They showed
us each in turn
That Water would certainly wet us, as Fire would certainly
burn:
But we found them lacking in Uplift, Vision and Breadth
of Mind,
So we left them to teach the Gorillas while we followed
the March of Mankind.

We moved as the Spirit listed. *They* never altered their
pace,
Being neither cloud nor wind-borne like the Gods of the
Market-Place;
But they always caught up with our progress, and presently
word would come
That a tribe had been wiped off its icefield, or the lights
had gone out in Rome.

With the Hopes that our World is built on they were
utterly out of touch,
They denied that the Moon was Stilton; they denied she
was even Dutch.
They denied that Wishes were Horses; they denied that a
Pig had Wings.
So we worshipped the Gods of the Market Who promised
these beautiful things.

When the Cambrian measures were forming, They
promised perpetual peace.
They swore, if we gave them our weapons, that the wars
of the tribes would cease.

But when we disarmed They sold us and delivered us
    bound to our foe,
And the Gods of the Copybook Headings said: *'Stick to the*
    Devil you know.'

On the first Feminian Sandstones we were promised the
    Fuller Life
(Which started by loving our neighbour and ended by
    loving his wife)
Till our women had no more children and the men lost
    reason and faith,
And the Gods of the Copybook Headings said: *'The Wages*
    of Sin is Death.'

In the Carboniferous Epoch we were promised abundance
    for all,
By robbing selected Peter to pay for collective Paul;
But, though we had plenty of money, there was nothing
    our money could buy,
And the Gods of the Copybook Headings said: *'If you*
    don't work you die.'

Then the Gods of the Market tumbled, and their smooth-
    tongued wizards withdrew,
And the hearts of the meanest were humbled and began to
    believe it was true
That All is not Gold that Glitters, and Two and Two
    make Four –
And the Gods of the Copybook Headings limped up to
    explain it once more.

★

As it will be in the future, it was at the birth of Man –
There are only four things certain since Social Progress
    began: –
That the Dog returns to his Vomit and the Sow returns to
    her Mire,
And the burnt Fool's bandaged finger goes wabbling back
    to the Fire;

And that after this is accomplished, and the brave new
  world begins
When all men are paid for existing and no man must pay
  for his sins,
As surely as Water will wet us, as surely as Fire will burn,
The Gods of the Copybook Headings with terror and
  slaughter return!

Rudyard Kipling
(1865–1936)

NIALL MCCARTHY
In Memory of Eva Gore-Booth and Con Markiewicz, W. B. Yeats

Dear Julie, Jonathan and Duncan,
Thank you for your letter, you compliment me. A favourite poem is 'In Memory of Eva Gore-Booth and Con Markiewicz' by W. B. Yeats. It is a poignant recall of a passing time, its later ravages, the withering of dreams and the arrested pictures of young beauty.

Good luck,
NIALL MCCARTHY

In Memory of Eva Gore-Booth and Con Markiewicz

The light of evening, Lissadell,
Great windows open to the south,
Two girls in silk kimonos, both
Beautiful, one a gazelle.

But a raving autumn shears
Blossom from the summer's wreath;
The older is condemned to death,
Pardoned, drags out lonely years
Conspiring among the ignorant.
I know not what the younger dreams —
Some vague Utopia — and she seems,
When withered old and skeleton-gaunt,
An image of such politics.
Many a time I think to seek
One or the other out and speak
Of that old Georgian mansion, mix
Pictures of the mind, recall
That table and the talk of youth,
Two girls in silk kimonos, both
Beautiful, one a gazelle.

Dear shadows, now you know it all,
All the folly of a fight
With a common wrong or right.
The innocent and the beautiful
Have no enemy but time;
Arise and bid me strike a match
And strike another till time catch;
Should the conflagration climb,
Run till all the sages know.
We the great gazebo built,
They convicted us of guilt;
Bid me strike a match and blow.

W. B. Yeats
(1865–1939)

SUE MILLER
The Old Fools, Philip Larkin

This poem seems remarkable to me in describing an alien state, in its use of language, and in its ability finally to force the reader into crossing some boundary between himself and 'the other' – in this case the old, the disoriented.

SUE MILLER

The Old Fools

What do they think has happened, the old fools,
To make them like this? Do they somehow suppose
It's more grown-up when your mouth hangs open and
    drools,
And you keep on pissing yourself, and can't remember
Who called this morning? Or that, if they only chose,
They could alter things back to when they danced all
    night,
Or went to their wedding, or sloped arms some
    September?
Or do they fancy there's really been no change,
And they've always behaved as if they were crippled or
    tight,
Or sat through days of thin continuous dreaming
Watching light move? If they don't (and they can't), it's
    strange:
                Why aren't they screaming?

At death, you break up: the bits that were you
Start speeding away from each other for ever
With no one to see. It's only oblivion, true:
We had it before, but then it was going to end,
And was all the time merging with a unique endeavour

To bring to bloom the million-petalled flower
Of being here. Next time you can't pretend
There'll be anything else. And these are the first signs:
Not knowing how, not hearing who, the power
Of choosing gone. Their looks show that they're for it:
Ash hair, toad hands, prune face dried into lines –
                How can they ignore it?

Perhaps being old is having lighted rooms
Inside your head, and people in them, acting.
People you know, yet can't quite name; each looms
Like a deep loss restored, from known doors turning,
Setting down a lamp, smiling from a stair, extracting
A known book from the shelves; or sometimes only
The rooms themselves, chairs and a fire burning,
The blown bush at the window, or the sun's
Faint friendliness on the wall some lonely
Rain-ceased midsummer evening. That is where they live:
Not here and now, but where all happened once.
              This is why they give

An air of baffled absence, trying to be there
Yet being here. For the rooms grow farther, leaving
Incompetent cold, the constant wear and tear
Of taken breath, and then crouching below
Extinction's alp, the old fools, never perceiving
How near it is. This must be what keeps them quiet:
The peak that stays in view wherever we go
For them is rising ground. Can they never tell
What is dragging them back, and how it will end? Not
   at night?
Not when the strangers come? Never, throughout
The whole hideous inverted childhood? Well
           We shall find out.

Philip Larkin
(1922–1985)

PADRAIC WHITE
Epic, Patrick Kavanagh
A Man I Knew, Brendan Kennelly

The universal greatness of Patrick Kavanagh.

I came to Dublin in 1960 to get my first job in the strange world to me of an 'office' in the big city of Dublin which was equally mysterious to me.

I was brought up in the peaceful village of Kinlough in County Leitrim and within walking distance of some beautiful countryside, lakes, rivers and ocean in Leitrim, Donegal and Sligo.

There was much talk in Dublin about Patrick Kavanagh at that time. He had come from a very rural part of Monaghan, was largely self-taught, and despite many vicissitudes of life was moved to write a great body of poetry and prose.

When I came to Dublin he wrote articles in newspapers for a part-living, was a well-known habitué of Baggot Street, its precincts and pubs. He died in 1967 at the age of sixty-two years.

I probably had a particular interest in his writing because I could identify with his rural background. With the passing of time, his true greatness becomes clearer.

I like Patrick Kavanagh's writing for two particular reasons, which my choice of poems illustrates. First, he could take small rural or everyday incidents and show their universal relevance as in the poem 'Epic'.

Epic

I have lived in important places, times
When great events were decided, who owned
That half a rood of rock, a no-man's land
Surrounded by our pitchfork-armed claims.
I heard the Duffys shouting 'Damn your soul'
And old McCabe stripped to the waist, seen
Step the plot defying blue cast-steel –
'Here is the march along these iron stones'.
That was the year of the Munich bother. Which
Was more important? I inclined

To lose my faith in Ballyrush and Gortin
Till Homer's ghost came whispering to my mind
He said: I made the Iliad from such
A local row. Gods make their own importance.

Patrick Kavanagh
(1904–1967)

Second, he was always true to himself and to the ultimate truth of life. This side of Kavanagh is beautifully illustrated in a poem about him entitled 'A Man I Knew – In Memory of Patrick Kavanagh' by Brendan Kennelly, who comes from Kerry, is an outstanding contemporary Irish poet and lectures at Trinity College Dublin.

Yours sincerely,
PADRAIC WHITE

A Man I Knew

(In memory of Patrick Kavanagh)

I

'I want no easy grave' he said to me,
'Where those who hated me can come and stare,
Slip down upon a servile knee,
Muttering their phoney public prayer.
In the wilds of Norfolk I'd like to lie,
No commemorative stone, no sheltering trees,
Far from the hypocrite's tongue and eye,
Safe from the praise of my enemies.'

A man I knew who seemed to me
The epitome of chivalry
Was constantly misunderstood.
The heart's dialogue with God
Was his life's theme and he
Explored its depths assiduously
And without rest. Therefore he spat
On every shoddy value that
Blinded men to their true destiny –
The evil power of mediocrity,
The safety of the barren pose,
All that distorted natural grace.
Which is to say, almost everything.
Once he asked a girl to sing
A medieval ballad. As her voice rang out,
She was affronted by some interfering lout.
This man I knew spat in his face
And wished him to the floor of hell.
I thought then, and still think it well
That man should wear the spittle of disgrace
For violating certain laws.
Now I recall my friend because
He lived according to his code
And in his way was true to God.
Courage he had and was content to be
Himself, whatever came his way.
There is no other chivalry.

Brendan Kennelly
(b. 1936)

MARY LAVIN
'I think continually of those who were truly great', Stephen Spender
Christ If You Wanted My Shining Soul, Mary Lavin

Dear Julie, and all you,
I am not sure if you want an attempt of my own at poetry or a poem by a real poet. To save time I am sending an effort of my own that I wrote long ago before the short story cast its spell over me.

I had spent far too long going over books of poetry until I realized that trying to make a striking choice was really a subtle form of vanity. Most of the poems that I found gave me the greatest joy were, oddly enough, those I had learned off by heart at school. Then suddenly I remembered a poem I first read in UCD which had stayed in my mind without my having consciously memorized it and I am sending it because it pays tribute to all the great poetry and prose that has sustained me throughout a long life, and probably had given me the impetus to dare to try writing myself, fairly late in life. Incidentally I have learned that the intoxication of writing comes from straining to write as well as one can and not from success.

Good luck,
MARY LAVIN

I think continually of those who were truly great.
Who, from the womb, remembered the soul's history
Through corridors of light where the hours are suns,
Endless and singing. Whose lovely ambition
Was that their lips, still touched with fire,
Should tell of the Spirit, clothed from head to foot in
    song.
And who hoarded from the Spring branches
The desires falling across their bodies like blossoms.

What is precious, is never to forget
The essential delight of the blood drawn from ageless
   springs
Breaking through rocks in worlds before our earth.
Never to deny its pleasure in the morning simple light
Nor its grave evening demand for love.
Never to allow gradually the traffic to smother
With noise and fog, the flowering of the Spirit.

Near the snow, near the sun, in the highest fields,
See how these names are fêted by the waving grass
And by the streamers of white cloud
And whispers of wind in the listening sky.
The names of those who in their lives fought for life,
Who wore at their hearts the fire's centre.
Born of the sun, they travelled a short while towards them
And left the vivid air signed with their honour.

Stephen Spender
(b. 1909)

Christ If You Wanted My Shining Soul

Christ if you wanted my shining soul
That flashed its happy fins
And splashed in the silent seas of sin,
Then Christ, keenest fisherman
On the Galilean shore,
If you wanted to catch my shivering soul
Why did you let down nets that were worn,
Unravelled and floating light?
I slid along the ribbony web
In and out
And when the nets slime-wet and black
Crawled over the prow of your boat again
Empty as nets that sway all day
In an empty sea

My sly soul waited
And swam aloft
To play at leaping the ripples
And showing its silver dapples
To the silently floating fishes
On the outer-side of the wave
The little silver minnows of the moon.

Mary Lavin
(b. 1912)

SR STANISLAUS KENNEDY
Street Corner Christ, Patrick Kavanagh

Dear Julie, Jonathan and Duncan,
'Street Corner Christ' is a poem very close to my own heart and, given the nature of your cause, I feel, an appropriate contribution. I have kept my comments to the bare minimum and although my few lines do not do justice to this poem it is my heartfelt wish that in helping to raise funds for Ethiopia they may allow justice to be done elsewhere.

'Street Corner Christ' by Patrick Kavanagh. At first reading, the reader is struck by the simple poignancy of this poem and touched by the sadness which tinges the poet's description of his subject matter – 'an uncouth ballad seller with tail-matted hair'.

But to be merely touched by the images which predominate the verse and not to recognize the harsh criticism which the poet is levelling at society, would not do Kavanagh justice. It would be similar in fact, to becoming 'as blind and deaf' as the 'pieties' within the poem whose narrowness of vision prohibits them from seeing the truth.

Indeed, acceptance of such criticism is integral to identifying with the poet and to understanding and empathizing with the *message* of the poem. It was Christ, after all, who said 'whatever you do to the least of these my brethren, you do unto me'. Surely, it follows, then, that if it takes a little bit of poetic licence to bring these words home to us and to help all those who seek to find their own street corner Christ in the 'rags of a beggar', then God Bless Paddy Kavanagh!

If there is any other way in which I can be of assistance please don't hesitate to contact me.

With kindest regards,

Yours sincerely,
SR STANISLAUS KENNEDY

Street Corner Christ

I saw Christ today
At a street corner stand,
In the rags of a beggar he stood
He held ballads in his hand.

He was crying out: 'Two for a penny
Will anyone buy
The finest ballads ever made
From the stuff of joy?'

But the blind and deaf went past
Knowing only there
An uncouth ballad seller
With tail-matted hair.

And I whom men call fool
His ballads bought,
Found Him whom the pieties
Have vainly sought.

Patrick Kavanagh
(1904–1967)

ELLEN GILCHRIST
Petition, W. H. Auden

Over the years lines from this poem have taught me different things at different times, and, always, as I grew older, it has reminded me to 'look shining at new styles of architecture, a change of heart'.

It has kept my heart from calcifying. The heart is very near the thymus gland, where the t-lymphocytes and killer glands of the immune system get their training. Very important to stay flexible in that area.

Also, if one is going to posit and address a higher being it should always be as sir or madam.

I loved *Lifelines I* and look forward to the new one.

All best wishes,
ELLEN GILCHRIST

Petition

Sir, no man's enemy, forgiving all
But will its negative inversion, be prodigal:
Send to us power and light, a sovereign touch
Curing the intolerable neural itch,
The exhaustion of weaning, the liar's quinsy,
And the distortions of ingrown virginity.
Prohibit sharply the rehearsed response
And gradually correct the coward's stance;
Cover in time with beams those in retreat
That, spotted, they turn though the reverse were great,
Publish each healer that in city lives
Or country houses at the end of drives;
Harrow the house of the dead; look shining at
New styles of architecture, a change of heart.

W. H. Auden
(1907–1973)

JUDI DENCH
Adlestrop, Edward Thomas

Dear Julie, Jonathan and Duncan,
I was so pleased to have your letter and to read about the book you are putting together. I am particularly pleased to be asked to contribute as both my parents went to Wesley College, and I have lovely memories of several visits to Dublin.

One of my favourite poems is 'Adlestrop' by Edward Thomas. I love it because of its essential Englishness and because it reminds me of the time of steam trains and that special hiss that announced their arrivals and departures. It is a very nostalgic poem about a part of England that I know well, and I hope its inclusion will introduce the poem to lots of new readers.

With best wishes,
JUDI DENCH

Adlestrop

Yes. I remember Adlestrop –
The name, because one afternoon
Of heat the express-train drew up there
Unwontedly. It was late June.

The steam hissed. Someone cleared his throat.
No one left and no one came
On the bare platform. What I saw
Was Adlestrop – only the name

And willows, willow-herb, and grass,
And meadowsweet, and haycocks dry,
No whit less still and lonely fair
Than the high cloudlets in the sky.

And for that minute a blackbird sang
Close by, and round him, mistier,
Farther and farther, all the birds
Of Oxfordshire and Gloucestershire.

Edward Thomas
(1878–1917)

RICHARD BRANSON
An Otter, Ted Hughes

Dear Julie, Jonathan and Duncan,
Richard has asked me to thank you for your letter. His favourite poem is
Ted Hughes's 'An Otter'. He loves otters!
  Hope you raise lots of money with your book!

Best wishes,
CLODAGH SIMONDS
Secretary to Richard Branson

An Otter

I

Underwater eyes, an eel's
Oil of water body, neither fish nor beast is the otter:
  Four-legged yet water-gifted, to outfish fish;
    With webbed feet and long ruddering tail
    And a round head like an old tomcat.

    Brings the legend of himself
From before wars or burials, in spite of hounds and
      vermin-poles;

Does not take root like the badger. Wanders, cries;
    Gallops along land he no longer belongs to;
    Re-enters the water by melting.

    Of neither water nor land. Seeking
Some world lost when first he dived, that he cannot come
       at since,
  Takes his changed body into the holes of lakes;
    As if blind, cleaves the stream's push till he licks
    The pebbles of the source; from sea

    To sea crosses in three nights
Like a king in hiding. Crying to the old shape of the starlit
      land,
  Over sunken farms where the bats go round,
    Without answer. Till light and birdsong come
    Walloping up roads with the milk wagon.

II

The hunt's lost him. Pads on mud,
Among sedges, nostrils a surface bead,
The otter remains, hours. The air,
Circling the globe, tainted and necessary,

Mingling tobacco-smoke, hounds and parsley,
Comes carefully to the sunk lungs.
So the self under the eye lies,
Attendant and withdrawn. The otter belongs

In double robbery and concealment —
From water that nourishes and drowns, and from land
That gave him his length and the mouth of the hound.
He keeps fat in the limpid integument

Reflections live on. The heart beats thick,
Big trout muscle out of the dead cold;
Blood is the belly of logic; he will lick
The fishbone bare. And can take stolen hold

On a bitch otter in a field full
Of nervous horses, but linger nowhere.
Yanked above hounds, reverts to nothing at all,
To this long pelt over the back of a chair.

Ted Hughes
(b. 1930)

CHAIM HERZOG
The Lake Isle of Innisfree, W. B. Yeats

Dear Julie, Jonathan and Duncan,
Many thanks for your letter dated January 1988. I am very happy to help you in your efforts to raise money for famine victims in Ethiopia. I congratulate you on the success of your efforts, following the production of *Lifelines I* and wish you every success in your further endeavours to help the starving people in the Third World.

It is very difficult, indeed, for me to choose a particular poem or poet. A very deep appreciation and love of poetry was instilled in me when I was a pupil at Wesley College. The result is that I have far too many favourite poets and favourite poems and it is, therefore, not easy for me to choose one. However, since I am contributing to an effort in Ireland let me say that one of my favourite poets is W. B. Yeats. His poem that has remained with me as a favourite is 'The Lake Isle of Innisfree'. I believe that few poems have given life to a rustic scene as has done this poem. Everything as it were comes to life – the beauty of the quietness of the glade in which he will build a small cabin, the bees, the cricket, the shimmer and glimmer of the morning and the night and the birds. All this against the background of the lake with the water lapping by the shores. Yeats was certainly one of the greatest poets of our time. He succeeded in his beautiful poems to bring to life so many aspects of nature, of life and of art. All this against the background of his deep love for Ireland and its legends and his idealistic devotion to the cause of the Irish Revolution. W. B. Yeats is, in my mind, a poet who will survive the ages and who belongs to eternity.

With best wishes,

Yours sincerely,
CHAIM HERZOG

The Lake Isle of Innisfree

I will arise and go now, and go to Innisfree,
And a small cabin build there, of clay and wattles made:
Nine bean-rows will I have there, a hive for the honey-
    bee,
And live alone in the bee-loud glade.

And I shall have some peace there, for peace comes
    dropping slow,
Dropping from the veils of the morning to where the
    cricket sings;
There midnight's all a glimmer, and noon a purple glow,
And evening full of the linnet's wings.

I will arise and go now, for always night and day
I hear lake water lapping with low sounds by the shore;
While I stand on the roadway, or on the pavements grey,
I hear it in the deep heart's core.

W. B. Yeats
(1865–1939)

CLARE BOYLAN
'The Bustle in a House',
Emily Dickinson

Dear Julie Grantham,
In reply to your request for a choice of poem for your anthology: I haven't
got a favourite poem but I like the work of Emily Dickinson because she
uses Victorian sentiment as a vehicle for irony and at the same time touches
the heart by connecting the ordinary and the domestic to the great
emotions.

The simple, untitled poem below (written in 1866) sets a scene which is recognizable to everybody and heightens the poignancy by wryly imposing the platitudes of outsiders upon the bereaved, for 'The sweeping up the heart and putting love away' is the hope of the comforter and not the reality for anyone who has lost someone they love.

I am sorry for the delay in replying to your request, but this is the first clear space I have had this year. I wish you every success with the venture.

With all good wishes,

Yours,
CLARE BOYLAN

The Bustle in a House
The Morning after Death
Is solemnest of industries
Enacted upon Earth –

The Sweeping up the Heart
And putting Love away
We shall not want to use again
Until Eternity.

Emily Dickinson
(1830–1886)

NUALA NÍ DHOMHNAILL
The Arrival of the Bee Box, Sylvia Plath
Antarctica, Derek Mahon

'The Arrival of the Bee Box': I have to confess that I chose this poem because I am a bit of a Sylvia Plath *affectionado*, especially of the later poems which many have termed hysterical, and self-dramatizing. I am not frightened or repelled by these powerful poems; rather I find they are the nearest thing I have ever read to some of my own states of mind, writ large. I read these poems as extremely honest and clear-eyed expressions of women's emotions in a society that frustrates the self-fulfilment of women. Literary critics, men for the most part, and especially covert upholders of the old order, are particularly baffled by these poems. They pretend to be irritated by them. Mostly, actually, they are frightened out of their skins.

For all its seeming artlessness, this poem is actually very finely crafted. Plath has come far from the careful, formal stylization of, say, 'The Colossus', but has lost nothing in transit. The poem fairly buzzes with energy, not the least of which is the energy of simple, colloquial words and phrases – 'coffin of a midget', 'a square baby', 'I have simply ordered a box of maniacs' – yet the whole is greater than the parts, being as it is, almost one long sustained metaphor. Muriel Rukeyser asked once:

> What would happen if one woman told the truth about her life?
> The world would split open.

In the terrible tension of containing the clamour of the host of my own interior selves, so as not to destroy the world, I am often that bee box. I am like a walking keg of dynamite. As in Plath's poem, a whole swarm of dark little angry things are barely contained within my skin. A great African Queen would loose her cohorts if I ever took the lid off. And nobody knows as well as I do how they can sting. It is perhaps interesting that the phrase used in Irish for acting on a sudden impulse is 'do phrioch an bheach mé' – 'the bee stung me'. In view of Sylvia Plath's untimely death the last line of the poem is particularly poignant and prophetic: 'The box is only temporary.' It would make you wonder if the price to pay for leaving all the bees out is always as great as it had to be in her case.

The Arrival of the Bee Box

I ordered this, this clean wood box
Square as a chair and almost too heavy to lift.
I would say it was the coffin of a midget
Or a square baby
Were there not such a din in it.

The box is locked, it is dangerous.
I have to live with it overnight
And I can't keep away from it,
There are no windows, so I can't see what is in there
There is only a little grid, no exit.

I put my eye to the grid.
It is dark, dark,
With the swarmy feeling of African hands
Minute and shrunk for export,
Black on black, angrily clambering.

How can I let them out?
It is the noise that appals me most of all,
The unintelligible syllables.
It is like a Roman mob,
Small, taken one by one, but my god, together!

I lay my ear to furious Latin.
I am not a Caesar.
I have simply ordered a box of maniacs.
They can be sent back.
They can die, I need feed them nothing, I am the owner.

I wonder how hungry they are.
I wonder if they would forget me
If I just undid the locks and stood back and turned into a
    tree.
There is the laburnum, its blond colonnades,
And the petticoats of the cherry.

They might ignore me immediately
In my moon suit and funeral veil.
I am no source of honey
So why should they turn on me?
Tomorrow I will be sweet God, I will set them free.

The box is only temporary.

Sylvia Plath
(1932–1963)

Now, just to show that I have no particular prejudice against formalism as
such, my second choice is, on the surface at least, a very different kind of
poem – Derek Mahon's 'Antarctica'. Once, before a reading, I asked Derek
to read this poem as a special favour and he said he felt a bit of a dolt

reading it, hearing all those rhymes and repetitions clanging heavily about his ears. But he still read it for me, and then I knew at once why I loved this poem, because it suddenly dawned on me that the dull thud of the repetitions is an absolutely intrinsic part of the poem itself. If every poem, as opposed to every piece of verse, is an invocation or an evocation of the Muse, then it must be the Goddess Durga who is called into being here, the Snow Queen, mistress of the cold impenetrable regions of the psyche, that inner tundra. It is a region I have travelled in myself, where the bouncing common-sense ego on which our civilization is built perishes in a vertiginous swoon. Therefore, as Derek Mahon says himself, this is a feminist poem, because it chronicles the moment when the more-than-faintly-ridiculous heroic male ego finally snuffs it. The rigidity of the metre and the constant repetitions are a very symptom of the state of the soul. The psyche is an ice-box, a house in mid winter with the heat turned off. In this state you wander about, metaphorically, in furs and high boots, in a frozen stupor, stamping your feet and repeating yourself constantly. The pipes, the conduits of emotion, are frozen solid, rigid like the lines of the poem. Thus for me, 'Antarctica' is the supreme example of a formal poem that is not merely emptily so, but where the metre and strict rhyming scheme play an essential part in building up the reality enacted.

> Ta súil agam go ndéanfaidh an méid seo cúis,
> NUALA X X X

Antarctica

'I am just going outside and may be some time.'
The others nod, pretending not to know.
At the heart of the ridiculous, the sublime.

He leaves them reading and begins to climb,
Goading his ghost into the howling snow;
He is just going outside and may be some time.

The tent recedes beneath its crust of rime
And frostbite is replaced by vertigo:
At the heart of the ridiculous, the sublime.

Need we consider it some sort of crime,
This numb self-sacrifice of the weakest? No,
He is just going outside and may be some time –

In fact, for ever. Solitary enzyme,
Though the night yield no glimmer there will glow,
At the heart of the ridiculous, the sublime.

He takes leave of the earthly pantomime
Quietly, knowing it is time to go: –
'I am just going outside and may be some time.'
At the heart of the ridiculous, the sublime.

Derek Mahon
(b. 1941)

ANTONY SHER
Sonnet 29, William Shakespeare

One of my favourite poems is Shakespeare's Sonnet 29, 'When, in disgrace with fortune and men's eyes'. It was a favourite piece of the actor Norman Henry, a dear friend and respected colleague in the Royal Shakespeare Company who sadly died last year. I read this sonnet at his memorial service at Trinity Church in Stratford-upon-Avon.

Good luck with the book,
ANTONY SHER

Sonnet 29

When, in disgrace with fortune and men's eyes,
I all alone beweep my outcast state,
And trouble deaf heaven with my bootless cries,
And look upon myself, and curse my fate,
Wishing me like to one more rich in hope,
Featured like him, like him with friends possessed,
Desiring this man's art and that man's scope,
With what I most enjoy contented least;

Yet in these thoughts myself almost despising,
Haply I think on thee – and then my state,
Like to the lark at break of day arising
From sullen earth, sings hymns at heaven's gate;
For thy sweet love rememb'red such wealth brings
That then I scorn to change my state with kings.

William Shakespeare
(1564–1616)

MARGARET ATWOOD
The Snowman, P. K. Page

Dear Lifelines,
Your efforts on behalf of starving people are most commendable. I don't
have one favourite poem – I have many – but I'm sending you this quite
wonderful poem by Canadian poet P. K. Page. You may not know the
poet or the poem – but both are well known here – and I have a particular
affection for this poem, having read it at an early age – and having built
many a snowman in my day!

With best wishes for your project,
MARGARET ATWOOD

The Snowman

Ancient nomadic snowman has rolled round.
His spoor: a wide swathe on the white ground
signs of a wintry struggle where he stands.

Stands? Yes, he stands. What snowman sat?
Legless, indeed, but more as if he had
legs than had not.

White double O, white nothing nothing, this
the child's first man on a white paper, his
earliest and fistful image is

now three-dimensional. Abstract. Everyman.
Of almost manna, he is still no man
no person, this so personal snowman.

O transient un-inhabitant, I know
no child who, on seeing the leprous thaw
undo your whitened torso and face of snow

would not, had he the magic
call you back
from that invisible attack

even knowing he can, with the new miracle
of another and softer and whiter snowfall
make you again, this time more wonderful.

Innocent single snowman. Overnight
brings him – a bright
omen – a thunderbolt of white.

But once I saw a mute in every yard
come like a plague; a stock-still multitude
and all stone-buttoned, bun-faced and absurd.

And next day they were still there but each
had changed a little as if all had inched
forward or back, I barely knew which;

and greyed a little too, grown sinister
and disreputable in their sooty fur,
numb, unmoving and nothing moving near.

And as far as I could see the snow was scarred
only with angels' wing marks or the feet of birds
like twigs broken upon the snow or shards

discarded. And I could hear no sound
as far as I could hear except a round
kind of echo without end

rung like a hoop below them and above
jarring the air they had no need of
in a landscape without love.

P. K. (Patricia Kathleen) Page
(b. 1916)

JEREMY IRONS
Apollinaire Said, Anonymous

Dear Joann, Jacki and Carolyn,
Thank you for your letter regarding *Lifelines III*. Herewith my poem, the author is unknown to me. It is my favourite poem since it deals with risk and trust and the magic that occurs sometimes when you do either.
  I hope this will suffice and I wish you good luck in your efforts.

Yours sincerely,
JEREMY IRONS

Apollinaire Said

Apollinaire said
'Come to the edge'
'It is too high'
'Come to the edge'
'We might fall'
'Come to the edge'
And they came
And he pushed them
And they flew

Anonymous

DESMOND HOGAN
My Teper' Ukhodim Ponemnogu,
Sergei Essenin

I have many favourite poems but in this evening's mood I mention this one, by Sergei Essenin, the Russian poet, husband of Isadora Duncan, who died young. It reminds me of his American contemporary Hart Crane. Both these young men, who don't look dissimilar – there is a wonderful letter by Hart Crane about a performance of Isadora Duncan's in Cleveland – are haunted by a sense of life's brevity and yet, as in this poem, are continually astonished by the loveliness of the earth, by what D. H. Lawrence called the 'God-flame', the 'fourth dimension', the part where mortal things encounter a sense of transcendence, a sense of ecstasy, a sense of connection, of not just holding hands but binding hands against thought and terror.

DESMOND HOGAN

My Teper' Ukhodim Ponemnogu

One by one we gradually are leaving
For the land of quietness and bliss.
Soon perhaps I also shall be needing
To embrace the hour of my release.

O beloved birch-trees of the forest!
Mother earth! You sands upon the plain!
Contemplating those who died before us
I can't hide my longing and my pain.

In this world I was too much enamoured
Of the things that make our soul enslaved.
May the aspens find a peace untrammelled
As they gaze into the rosy waves.

Many thoughts in silence I have pondered,
Many songs I quietly conceived,
And upon this dark and gloomy planet
I am happy that I lived and breathed.

I am happy that I fondled women,
Crumpled flowers and tumbled in the grass,
And that animals, our little brethren,
Never felt the anger of my palms.

I'm aware that there we'll find no forest,
And no ringing of the swan-necked rye.
That is why all those who died before us
Always chill my heart until I cry.

I'm aware there won't be any meadows
Glowing golden in that misty land.
That is why the people are so precious
Who on earth walk with me hand in hand.

> Sergei Essenin
> (1895–1925)
> (Translated by Gordon McVay)

(*My teper' ukhodim ponemnogu*: 'We are bound for the land of
the pure and the holy.' Literally it means 'We are leaving slowly
on the journey.')

A. S. BYATT
The Garden, Andrew Marvell

Dear Lifelines,
I am sorry not to have replied to your letter sooner but I have been abroad
and also overwhelmed with work.

My favourite poem (or one of my favourite poems) is Andrew Marvell's
'The Garden'. I love it because of its wit, its clarity, its image of perfect

vegetable peacefulness and the way it seems as new and surprising today as it must have done when it was written. I have always for some reason been drawn to images of the Paradise Garden and this is one of the most subtle and the most beautiful.

Yours sincerely,
A. S. BYATT

The Garden

I

How vainly men themselves amaze
To win the palm, the oak, or bays,
And their uncessant labours see
Crowned from some single herb or tree,
Whose short and narrow vergèd shade
Does prudently their toils upbraid,
While all flow'rs and all trees do close
To weave the garlands of repose.

II

Fair Quiet, have I found thee here,
And Innocence, thy sister dear!
Mistaken long, I sought you then
In busy companies of men.
Your sacred plants, if here below,
Only among the plants will grow.
Society is all but rude,
To this delicious solitude.

III

No white nor red was ever seen
So am'rous as this lovely green.
Fond lovers, cruel as their flame,
Cut in these trees their mistress' name.
Little, alas, they know, or heed,
How far these beauties hers exceed!
Fair trees! wheres'e'er your barks I wound,
No name shall but your own be found.

IV

When we have run our passion's heat,
Love hither makes his best retreat.
The gods, that mortal beauty chase,
Still in a tree did end their race.
Apollo hunted Daphne so,
Only that she might laurel grow.
And Pan did after Syrinx speed,
Not as a nymph, but for a reed.

V

What wondrous life is this I lead!
Ripe apples drop about my head;
The luscious clusters of the vine
Upon my mouth do crush their wine;
The nectarene, and curious peach,
Into my hands themselves do reach;
Stumbling on melons, as I pass,
Ensnared with flowers, I fall on grass.

VI

Meanwhile the mind, from pleasures less,
Withdraws into its happiness:
The mind, that ocean where each kind
Does straight its own resemblance find,
Yet it creates, transcending these,
Far other worlds, and other seas,
Annihilating all that's made
To a green thought in a green shade.

VII

Here at the fountain's sliding foot,
Or at some fruit-tree's mossy root,
Casting the body's vest aside,
My soul into the boughs does glide:
There like a bird it sits, and sings,
Then whets, and combs its silver wings;
And, till prepared for longer flight,
Waves in its plumes the various light.

VIII

Such was that happy garden-state,
While man there walked without a mate:
After a place so pure, and sweet,
What other help could yet be meet!
But 'twas beyond a mortal's share
To wander solitary there:
Two paradises 'twere in one
To live in paradise alone.

IX

How well the skilful gardener drew
Of flowers and herbs this dial new;
Where from above the milder sun
Does through a fragrant zodiac run;
And, as it works, the industrious bee
Computes its time as well as we.
How could such sweet and wholesome hours
Be reckoned but with herbs and flowers!

Andrew Marvell
(1621–1678)

DAVID OWEN
Candles, C. P. Cavafy

Dear Lifelines,
Thank you for your letter about your project *Lifelines*, and I am sorry to
have not replied before now. In fact I have been busy myself producing an
anthology of poetry which is to be published in the autumn by Michael
Joseph, the proceeds of which will be donated to Great Ormond Street
Hospital.

I wish you success in your fundraising efforts with *Lifelines* to raise funds for the Third World.

My favourite poem is 'Candles' by C. P. Cavafy, translated by Rae Dalven. It is a reminder that so many things in life fade or die and that you must always look forward, not back. In politics, particularly, there is a need to move on, learn from past mistakes or achievements; but don't dwell in the past, live for the future. I have found Rae Dalven's translation of the Greek poet's work particularly beautiful.

Yours sincerely,
DAVID OWEN
The Rt Hon The Lord Owen

Candles

The days of our future stand before us
like a row of little lighted candles –
golden, warm, and lively little candles.

The days gone by remain behind us,
a mournful line of burnt-out candles;
the nearest ones are still smoking,
cold candles, melted and bent.

I do not want to look at them; their form saddens me,
and it saddens me to recall their first light.
I look ahead at my lighted candles.

I do not want to turn back, lest I see and shudder –
how quickly the sombre line lengthens,
how quickly the burnt-out candles multiply.

C. P. Cavafy
(1863–1933)
(Translated by Rae Dalven)

JAMES PLUNKETT
In Memory of My Mother, Patrick Kavanagh

Who my favourite poet is, and what is my favourite poem, are questions to be sidestepped as nimbly as good manners permit: the answers vary almost from moment to moment. However, Patrick Kavanagh and the poems of Patrick Kavanagh occupy an elevated place in the list at all times.

I came to know of him first in the 1940s when I read his epic poem *The Great Hunger* and then in person when I met him during the fifties in the company of Peadar O'Donnell, who was editing *The Bell* at the time. After that there were casual meetings in the coffee shops of Bewleys and Mitchells and in Sunday pubs. His work, in both prose and poetry, became a must.

The poem I have selected here is from *Come Dance with Kitty Stobling and Other Poems*, first published in 1960. It is 'In Memory of My Mother'. I found it deeply moving when I first read it and it continues to evoke the same admiration and emotion whenever I return to it, especially on the repetition at the beginning of the last verse of the line:

> O you are not lying in the wet clay . . .

What a tender, brooding sorrow hovers over it.

With good wishes for the success of *Lifelines III*.

Sincerely,
JAMES PLUNKETT

In Memory of My Mother

I do not think of you lying in the wet clay
Of a Monaghan graveyard; I see
You walking down a lane among the poplars
On your way to the station, or happily

Going to second Mass on a summer Sunday –
You meet me and you say:
'Don't forget to see about the cattle –'
Among your earthiest words the angels stray.

And I think of you walking along a headland
Of green oats in June,
So full of repose, so rich with life –
And I see us meeting at the end of a town

On a fair day by accident, after
The bargains are all made and we can walk
Together through the shops and stalls and markets
Free in the oriental streets of thought.

O you are not lying in the wet clay,
For it is a harvest evening now and we
Are piling up the ricks against the moonlight
And you smile up at us – eternally.

Patrick Kavanagh
(1904–1967)

ADAM CLAYTON
Rock, Charles Bukowski

Dear Lifelines,
Thank you for your letter. I enclose a copy of Adam's chosen poem:
'Rock' by Charles Bukowski, an American writer on rock musicians.
  With best wishes,

Yours sincerely,
SUZANNE DOYLE

Rock

Here were all these males tuning their guitars
not a woman around
and they were content with that.

Then they started arguing about who was best
and what was wrong with the so called best:
and a couple of them had been famous,
and they sat there on my rug
drinking my wine and beer and smoking my cigarettes.

Two of them stood up to duke it out
and that's when I ran them off
with their guitars and their guitar cases
out into the moonlight
still arguing.

I closed the door then I leaned against the couch
and drained a beer fast and I gagged:
not a very good night:
it was full of ashes.

Charles Bukowski
(b. 1920)

IAN MCKELLEN
The Leaden Echo and the Golden Echo, Gerard Manley Hopkins

Dear Joann Bradish,
My favourite poem, perhaps, is by G. M. Hopkins – 'The Leaden Echo and the Golden Echo'.

I admire Hopkins's use of language, strongly influenced by Shakespeare's use of punning and metaphor. These lines were originally intended to be part of a dramatic work and, when spoken out loud, reveal a wonderful grasp of theatrical passion. Although I am not Christian, I always find the optimism of the second part of the poem very moving indeed.

All best wishes to you and to Jacki Erskine and to Carolyn Gibson.

Yours ever,
IAN MCKELLEN

The Leaden Echo and the Golden Echo

(Maiden's song from *St Winefred's Well*)

The Leaden Echo

How to kéep – is there ány any, is there none such,
  nowhere known some, bow or brooch or braid or
  brace, láce, latch or catch or key to keep
Back beauty, keep it, beauty, beauty, beauty, . . . from
  vanishing away?
Ó is there no frowning of these wrinkles, rankèd wrinkles
  deep,
Dówn? no waving off of these most mournful messengers,
  still messengers, sad and stealing messengers of grey?
No there's none, there's none, O no there's none,
Nor can you long be, what you now are, called fair,
Do what you may do, what, do what you may,
And wisdom is early to despair:
Be beginning; since, no, nothing can be done
To keep at bay
Age and age's evils, hoar hair,
Ruck and wrinkle, drooping, dying, death's worst,
  winding sheets, tombs and worms and tumbling to
  decay;
So be beginning, be beginning to despair.
O there's none; no no no there's none:
Be beginning to despair, to despair,
Despair, despair, despair, despair.

The Golden Echo

  Spare!
There ís one, yes I have one (Hush there!);
Only not within seeing of the sun,
Not within the singeing of the strong sun,
Tall sun's tingeing, or treacherous the tainting of the
  earth's air,

Somewhere elsewhere there is ah well where! one,

Ońe. Yes I cán tell such a key, I dó know such a place,

Where whatever's prized and passes of us, everything
    that's fresh and fast flying of us, seems to us sweet of us
    and swiftly away with, done away with, undone,

Úndone, done with, soon done with, and yet dearly and
    dangerously sweet

Of us, the wimpled-water-dimpled, not-by-morning-
    matchèd face,

The flower of beauty, fleece of beauty, too too apt to, ah!
    to fleet,

Never fleets móre, fastened with the tenderest truth

To its own best being and its loveliness of youth: it is an
    everlastingness of, O it is an all youth!

Come then, your ways and airs and looks, locks, maiden
    gear, gallantry and gaiety and grace,

Winning ways, airs innocent, maiden manners, sweet
    looks, loose locks, long locks, lovelocks, gaygear, going
    gallant, girlgrace –

Resign them, sign them, seal them, send them, motion
    them with breath,

And with sighs soaring, soaring síghs deliver

Them; beauty-in-the-ghost, deliver it, early now, long
    before death

Give beauty back, beauty, beauty, beauty, back to God,
    beauty's self and beauty's giver.

See; not a hair is, not an eyelash, not the least lash lost;
    every hair

Is, hair of the head, numbered.

Nay, what we had lighthanded left in surly the mere mould

Will have waked and have waxed and have walked with
    the wind what while we slept,

This side, that side hurling a heavyheaded hundredfold

What while we, while we slumbered.

O then, weary then whý should we tread? O why are we
    so haggard at the heart, so care-coiled, care-killed, so
    fagged, so fashed, so cogged, so cumbered,

When the thing we freely forfeit is kept with fonder a care,

Fonder a care kept than we could have kept it, kept
Far with fonder a care (and we, we should have lost it)
   finer, fonder
A care kept. – Where kept? Do but tell us where kept,
   where. –
Yonder. – What high as that! We follow, now we
   follow. –
   Yonder, yes yonder, yonder,
Yonder.

Gerard Manley Hopkins
(1844–1889)

FIONA SHAW
The Song of Wandering Aengus,
W. B. Yeats
The Second Coming, W. B. Yeats

Dear Joann, Jacki and Carolyn,
Thank you so very much for inviting me to be part of your anthology. I am truly honoured particularly as I think your predecessors asked me and due to my infinite moves my reply was never sent.

Anyway, good luck with this and I do hope it's another sell-out.

You have asked a difficult question. 'Favourite' is always hard for a fanatic, so I have approached this by trying to narrow down the possibilities to a favourite poet.

I have decided that it is Yeats and I am full of trepidation that too many of your poems will be Yeats choices. Mine is either: 'The Song of Wandering Aengus' and I really don't know why. I don't intellectually understand the poem but I think it's great because the moment you start reading it you are transported to another place, the inside of someone else's vision and you travel swiftly through landscape and time even to the end of life with the yearning speaker and then you wake up at the end of the poem having had the beatific rest of unravelling sleep.

If too many chose that poem I would like to offer the alternative of 'The Second Coming'. I love this poem because it frightens me!

Best wishes,

Yours, with gratitude,
FIONA SHAW

The Song of Wandering Aengus

I went out to the hazel wood,
Because a fire was in my head,
And cut and peeled a hazel wand,
And hooked a berry to a thread;
And when white moths were on the wing,
And moth-like stars were flickering out,
I dropped the berry in a stream
And caught a little silver trout.

When I had laid it on the floor
I went to blow the fire aflame,
But something rustled on the floor,
And some one called me by my name:
It had become a glimmering girl
With apple blossom in her hair
Who called me by my name and ran
And faded through the brightening air.

Though I am old with wandering
Through hollow lands and hilly lands,
I will find out where she has gone,
And kiss her lips and take her hands;
And walk among long dappled grass,
And pluck till time and times are done
The silver apples of the moon,
The golden apples of the sun.

W. B. Yeats
(1865–1939)

The Second Coming

Turning and turning in the widening gyre
The falcon cannot hear the falconer;
Things fall apart; the centre cannot hold;
Mere anarchy is loosed upon the world,
The blood-dimmed tide is loosed, and everywhere
The ceremony of innocence is drowned;
The best lack all conviction, while the worst
Are full of passionate intensity.

Surely some revelation is at hand;
Surely the Second Coming is at hand.
The Second Coming! Hardly are those words out
When a vast image out of *Spiritus Mundi*
Troubles my sight: somewhere in sands of the desert
A shape with lion body and the head of a man,
A gaze blank and pitiless as the sun,
Is moving its slow thighs, while all about it
Reel shadows of the indignant desert birds.
The darkness drops again; but now I know
That twenty centuries of stony sleep
Were vexed to nightmare by a rocking cradle,
And what rough beast, its hour come round at last,
Slouches towards Bethlehem to be born?

W. B. Yeats
(1865–1939)

KINGSLEY AMIS
Last Poems, XL, A. E. Housman

Dear Misses Bradish, Erskine and Gibson,
Thank you for your letter about *Lifelines*. My favourite poem is by A. E. Housman. It has no title but the first line is:

Tell me not here, it needs not saying,

Why is it my favourite poem? I am afraid I would have to know much more about myself than I do to answer that question. But I can say that it is a piece of beautiful observation, precisely expressed and it exactly expresses what I have myself sometimes felt in rural places. I wish you the best of luck with *Lifelines III*.

Yours sincerely,
KINGSLEY AMIS

Last Poems

XL

Tell me not here, it needs not saying,
    What tune the enchantress plays
In aftermaths of soft September
    Or under blanching mays,
For she and I were long acquainted
    And I knew all her ways.

On russet floors, by waters idle,
    The pine lets fall its cone;
The cuckoo shouts all day at nothing
    In leafy dells alone;
And traveller's joy beguiles in autumn
    Hearts that have lost their own.

On acres of the seeded grasses
   The changing burnish heaves;
Or marshalled under moons of harvest
   Stand still all night the sheaves;
Or beeches strip in storms for winter
   And stain the wind with leaves.

Possess, as I possessed a season,
   The countries I resign,
Where over elmy plains the highway
   Would mount the hills and shine,
And full of shade the pillared forest
   Would murmur and be mine.

For nature, heartless, witless nature,
   Will neither care nor know
What stranger's feet may find the meadow
   And trespass there and go,
Nor ask amid the dews of morning
   If they are mine or no.

A. E. Housman
(1859–1936)

AMY CLAMPITT
Jabberwocky, Lewis Carroll

Dear Joann Bradish, Jacki Erskine, and Carolyn Gibson,
You ask me to name my favorite poem. Like many other people, I have
too many favorites to settle for very long on any single one. But since I
first encountered it at the age of four or five, one of those favorites has
always been 'Jabberwocky' from *Through the Looking-Glass*, the second of
the Alice books by Lewis Carroll. It is one of the few poems I can recite

from memory without stumbling, and that is strange since it is studded with words that came out of nowhere and mean nothing in particular. As Alice herself put it, 'it seems to fill my head with ideas – only I don't know exactly what they are'. Anyhow, the sound of those words is somehow magical and ridiculous both at once. And the sound, after all, is what makes a good poem worth remembering.

Sincerely yours,
AMY CLAMPITT

Jabberwocky

'Twas brillig, and the slithy toves
    Did gyre and gimble in the wabe:
All mimsy were the borogoves,
    And the mome raths outgrabe.

'Beware the Jabberwock, my son!
    The jaws that bite, the claws that catch!
Beware the Jubjub bird, and shun
    The frumious Bandersnatch!'

He took his vorpal sword in hand:
    Long time the manxome foe he sought –
So rested he by the Tumtum tree,
    And stood awhile in thought.

And, as in uffish thought he stood,
    The Jabberwock, with eyes of flame,
Came whiffling through the tulgey wood,
    And burbled as it came!

One, two! One, two! And through and through
    The vorpal blade went snicker-snack!
He left it dead, and with its head
    He went galumphing back.

'And, hast thou slain the Jabberwock?
    Come to my arms, my beamish boy!
O frabjous day! Callooh! Callay!'
    He chortled in his joy.

'Twas brillig, and the slithy toves
   Did gyre and gimble in the wabe:
All mimsy were the borogoves,
   And the mome raths outgrabe.

Lewis Carroll
(1832–1898)

DAVID LODGE
Among School Children, W. B. Yeats

Dear Misses Bradish, Erskine and Gibson,
I would nominate as my favourite poem 'Among School Children' by
W. B. Yeats. It deals with some of the most fundamental human emotions:
love, nostalgia, regret, and the longing for what Yeats called elsewhere
'unity of being', but which he figured here in the wonderful final stanzas in
the symbols of the chestnut tree and the dancer. What I particularly admire
about the poem is the extraordinary range of diction, from the most down-
to-earth and colloquial, to the most sublime; and the way a natural-seeming
utterance is fitted into a most complex stanzaic form.

Yours sincerely,
DAVID LODGE

Among School Children

I

I walk through the long schoolroom questioning;
A kind old nun in a white hood replies;
The children learn to cipher and to sing,
To study reading-books and histories,
To cut and sew, be neat in everything

In the best modern way – the children's eyes
In momentary wonder stare upon
A sixty-year-old smiling public man.

II
I dream of a Ledaean body, bent
Above a sinking fire, a tale that she
Told of a harsh reproof, or trivial event
That changed some childish day to tragedy –
Told, and it seemed that our two natures blent
Into a sphere from youthful sympathy,
Or else, to alter Plato's parable,
Into the yolk and white of the one shell.

III
And thinking of that fit of grief or rage
I look upon one child or t'other there
And wonder if she stood so at that age –
For even daughters of the swan can share
Something of every paddler's heritage –
And had that colour upon cheek or hair,
And thereupon my heart is driven wild:
She stands before me as a living child.

IV
Her present image floats into the mind –
Did Quattrocento finger fashion it
Hollow of cheek as though it drank the wind
And took a mess of shadows for its meat?
And I though never of Ledaean kind
Had pretty plumage once – enough of that,
Better to smile on all that smile, and show
There is a comfortable kind of old scarecrow.

V
What youthful mother, a shape upon her lap
Honey of generation had betrayed,
And that must sleep, shriek, struggle to escape
As recollection or the drug decide,

Would think her son, did she but see that shape
With sixty or more winters on its head,
A compensation for the pang of his birth,
Or the uncertainty of his setting forth?

VI

Plato thought nature but a spume that plays
Upon a ghostly paradigm of things;
Solider Aristotle played the taws
Upon the bottom of a king of kings;
World-famous golden-thighed Pythagoras
Fingered upon a fiddle-stick or strings
What a star sang and careless Muses heard:
Old clothes upon old sticks to scare a bird.

VII

Both nuns and mothers worship images,
But those the candles light are not as those
That animate a mother's reveries,
But keep a marble or a bronze repose.
And yet they too break hearts – O Presences
That passion, piety or affection knows,
And that all heavenly glory symbolise –
O self-born mockers of man's enterprise;

VIII

Labour is blossoming or dancing where
The body is not bruised to pleasure soul,
Nor beauty born out of its own despair,
Nor blear-eyed wisdom out of midnight oil.
O chestnut-tree, great-rooted blossomer,
Are you the leaf, the blossom or the bole?
O body swayed to music, O brightening glance,
How can we know the dancer from the dance?

W. B. Yeats
(1865–1939)

BRYAN MACMAHON
Pádraic Ó Conaire, Gaelic Storyteller,
F. R. Higgins

Selecting one poem from a lifetime of reading poetry can be difficult. 'Byzantium', by W. B. Yeats, though incompletely understood, acts on my imagination like fire.

However, I tend to forsake the Middle East in favour of the Irish West. From there I select 'Pádraic Ó Conaire, Gaelic Storyteller' by F. R. Higgins. This is a poem I find myself chanting on the most unlikely occasions and to an audience only of myself.

The poet, now buried in Laracor in County Meath, imagines himself alone in the wake room where Sean-Phádraic is laid out. The other mourners have gone: alone, Higgins remains beside the corpse until the break of a cold dawn.

For me the poem is full of the nostalgic memory of oldsters telling me that they knew Sean-Phádraic, the picaresque personality who, with Pádraic Pearse, brought a new measure of reality to literature in Irish.

Again I hear the voices of those oldsters telling me of the rambler tying his Kinvara-bought donkey to a pole outside a pub in the Coombe or climbing the railings of the Park in St Stephen's Green to bed down among the ducks on the little island in the lake.

Image piles on vivid image as I recite. I observe the sea-cold eyes of the old writer, hear the tap of his heavy stick, find the west in his soft speech, or watch him step through the Spanish Arch in Galway City. I seem to see him 'exploring' the countryside: I also meet his comrades 'to whom our heights of race belong' – men who practise 'the secret joinery of song'.

Finally, I am back again in the wake room as the candlelight fades with the coming of morning. 'Death mars the parchment' of the old writer's forehead while the poet drinks to his eternal peace for the last time.

The funeral dirge is chanted by young winds rising on the barren countryside.

I strongly recommend the learning of this poem by heart.

I am certain that by doing so the student will gain a comrade for life.

With compliments agus le dea-mhéin,
BRYAN MACMAHON

They've paid the last respects in sad tobacco
And silent is this wakehouse in its haze;
They've paid the last respects; and now their whiskey
Flings laughing words on mouths of prayer and praise;
And so young couples huddle by the gables,
O let them grope home through the hedgy night –
Alone I'll mourn my old friend, while the cold dawn
Thins out the holy candlelight.

Respects are paid to one loved by the people;
Ah, was he not – among our mighty poor –
The sudden wealth cast on those pools of darkness,
Those bearing, just, a star's faint signature;
And so he was to me, close friend, near brother,
Dear Pádraic of the wide and sea-cold eyes –
So lovable, so courteous and noble,
The very West was in his soft replies.

They'll miss his heavy stick and stride in Wicklow –
His story-talking down Winetavern Street,
Where old men sitting in the wizen daylight
Have kept an edge upon his gentle wit;
While women on the grassy streets of Galway,
Who hearken for his passing – but in vain,
Shall hardly tell his steps as shadows vanish
Through archways of forgotten Spain.

Ah, they'll say: Pádraic's gone again exploring;
But now down glens of brightness, O he'll find
An alehouse overflowing with wise Gaelic
That's braced in vigour by the bardic mind,
And there his thoughts shall find their own forefathers –
In minds to whom our heights of race belong,
In crafty men, who ribbed a ship or turned
The secret joinery of song.

Alas, death mars the parchment of his forehead;
And yet for him, I know, the earth is mild –
The windy fidgets of September grasses
Can never tease a mind that loved the wild;
So drink his peace – this grey juice of the barley
Runs with a light that ever pleased his eye –
While old flames nod and gossip on the hearthstone
And only the young winds cry.

F. R. Higgins
(1896–1941)

BARBARA BUSH
From *Ode – Intimations of Immortality from Recollections of Early Childhood*, William Wordsworth

Dear Friends,
On behalf of Mrs Bush, thank you for your message. She appreciates your interest.

Mrs Bush has always enjoyed the works of William Wordsworth, especially his 'Ode – Intimations of Immortality from Recollections of Early Childhood'.

I know Mrs Bush would want me to convey her best wishes.

Sincerely,
JOAN C. DECAIN
Director of Correspondence for Mrs Bush

From *Ode – Intimations of Immortality from Recollections of Early Childhood*

The Child is father of the Man;
And I could wish my days to be
Bound each to each by natural piety.

I

There was a time when meadow, grove, and stream,
The earth, and every common sight,
      To me did seem
    Apparelled in celestial light,
The glory and the freshness of a dream.
It is not now as it hath been of yore –
    Turn whereso'er I may,
      By night or day,
The things which I have seen I now can see no more.

II

    The Rainbow comes and goes,
    And lovely is the Rose,
    The Moon doth with delight
Look round her when the heavens are bare,
      Waters on a starry night
      Are beautiful and fair;
    The sunshine is a glorious birth;
    But yet I know, where'er I go,
That there hath passed away a glory from the earth.

V

Our birth is but a sleep and a forgetting:
The Soul that rises with us, our life's Star,
    Hath had elsewhere its setting,
      And cometh from afar:
    Not in entire forgetfulness,
    And not in utter nakedness,
But trailing clouds of glory do we come
    From God, who is our home:

Heaven lies about us in our infancy!
Shades of the prison-house begin to close
    Upon the growing Boy,
       But He
Beholds the light, and whence it flows,
    He sees it in his joy;
The Youth, who daily farther from the east
    Must travel, still is Nature's Priest,
    And by the vision splendid
    Is on his way attended;
At length the Man perceives it die away,
And fade into the light of common day.

XI

And O, ye Fountains, Meadows, Hills and Groves,
Forbode not any severing of our loves!
Yet in my heart of hearts I feel your might;
I only have relinquished one delight
To live beneath your more habitual sway.
I love the Brooks which down their channels fret,
Even more than when I tripped lightly as they;
The innocent brightness of a newborn Day
    Is lovely yet;
The Clouds that gather round the setting sun
Do take a sober colouring from an eye
That hath kept watch o'er man's mortality;
Another race hath been, and other palms are won.
Thanks to the human heart by which we live,
Thanks to its tenderness, its joys, and fears,
To me the meanest flower that blows can give
Thoughts that do often lie too deep for tears.

               William Wordsworth
               (1770–1850)

WILLIAM TREVOR
The Lady of Shalott,
Alfred, Lord Tennyson

'The Lady of Shalott' is one of the poems I most enjoy, but to attempt to explain why that is would be like trying to explain why a certain food is a particular favourite. You cannot describe the taste of bananas or fresh peas. You cannot describe the magic of poetry.

Best wishes for your splendid project.
WILLIAM TREVOR

The Lady of Shalott

PART I

On either side the river lie
Long fields of barley and of rye,
That clothe the wold and meet the sky;
And through the field the road runs by
   To many-towered Camelot;
And up and down the people go,
Gazing where the lilies blow
Round an island there below,
   The island of Shalott.

Willows whiten, aspens quiver,
Little breezes dusk and shiver
Through the wave that runs forever
By the island in the river
   Flowing down to Camelot.
Four grey walls, and four grey towers,
Overlook a space of flowers,
And the silent isle imbowers
   The Lady of Shalott.

By the margin, willow-veiled,
Slide the heavy barges trailed
By slow horses; and unhailed
The shallop flitteth silken-sailed
   Skimming down to Camelot:
But who hath seen her wave her hand?
Or at the casement seen her stand?
Or is she known in all the land,
   The Lady of Shalott?

Only reapers, reaping early
In among the bearded barley,
Hear a song that echoes cheerly
From the river winding clearly,
   Down to towered Camelot;
And by the moon the reaper weary,
Piling sheaves in uplands airy,
Listening, whispers 'Tis the fairy
   Lady of Shalott.'

PART II

There she weaves by night and day
A magic web with colours gay.
She has heard a whisper say,
A curse is on her if she stay
   To look down to Camelot.
She knows not what the curse may be,
And so she weaveth steadily,
And little other care hath she,
   The Lady of Shalott.

And moving through a mirror clear
That hangs before her all the year,
Shadows of the world appear.
There she sees the highway near
   Winding down to Camelot;
There the river eddy whirls,
And there the surly village-churls,
And the red cloaks of market girls,
   Pass onward from Shalott.

Sometimes a troop of damsels glad,
An abbot on an ambling pad,
Sometimes a curly shepherd-lad
Or long-haired page in crimson clad,
   Goes by to towered Camelot;
And sometimes through the mirror blue
The knights come riding two and two:
She hath no loyal knight and true,
   The Lady of Shalott.

But in her web she still delights
To weave the mirror's magic sights,
For often through the silent nights
A funeral, with plumes and lights,
   And music, went to Camelot;
Or when the moon was overhead,
Came two young lovers lately wed;
'I am half sick of shadows,' said
   The Lady of Shalott.

PART III

A bowshot from her bower-eaves,
He rode between the barley-sheaves,
The sun came dazzling through the leaves,
And flamed upon the brazen greaves
   Of bold Sir Lancelot.
A red-cross knight forever kneeled
To a lady in his shield,
That sparkled on the yellow field,
   Beside remote Shalott.

The gemmy bridle glittered free,
Like to some branch of stars we see
Hung in the golden Galaxy.
The bridle bells rang merrily
   As he rode down to Camelot;
And from his blazoned baldric slung
A mighty silver bugle hung,
And as he rode his armour rung,
   Beside remote Shalott.

All in the blue unclouded weather
Thick-jewelled shone the saddle-leather,
The helmet and the helmet-feather
Burned like one burning flame together,
    As he rode down to Camelot;
As often through the purple night,
Below the starry clusters bright,
Some bearded meteor, trailing light,
    Moves over still Shalott.

His broad clear brow in sunlight glowed;
On burnished hooves his war-horse trode;
From underneath his helmet flowed
His coal-black curls as on he rode,
    As he rode down to Camelot.
From the bank and from the river
He flashed into the crystal mirror,
'Tirra lirra,' by the river
    Sang Sir Lancelot.

She left the web, she left the loom,
She made three paces through the room,
She saw the water-lily bloom,
She saw the helmet and the plume,
    She looked down to Camelot.
Out flew the web and floated wide;
The mirror cracked from side to side;
'The curse is come upon me,' cried
    The Lady of Shalott.

PART IV

In the stormy east-wind straining,
The pale yellow woods were waning,
The broad stream in his banks complaining,
Heavily the low sky raining
    Over towered Camelot;
Down she came and found a boat
Beneath a willow left afloat,
And round about the prow she wrote
    The Lady of Shalott.

And down the river's dim expanse –
Like some bold seër in a trance,
Seeing all his own mischance –
With a glassy countenance
    Did she look to Camelot.
And at the closing of the day
She loosed the chain, and down she lay;
The broad stream bore her far away,
    The Lady of Shalott.

Lying, robed in snowy white
That loosely flew to left and right –
The leaves upon her falling light –
Through the noises of the night
    She floated down to Camelot;
And as the boat-head wound along
The willowy hills and fields among,
They heard her singing her last song,
    The Lady of Shalott.

Heard a carol, mournful, holy,
Chanted loudly, chanted lowly,
Till her blood was frozen slowly,
And her eyes were darkened wholly,
    Turned to towered Camelot;
For ere she reached upon the tide
The first house by the waterside,
Singing in her song she died,
    The Lady of Shalott.

Under tower and balcony,
By garden-wall and gallery,
A gleaming shape she floated by,
Dead-pale between the houses high,
    Silent into Camelot.
Out upon the wharfs they came,
Knight and burgher, lord and dame,
And round the prow they read her name,
    The Lady of Shalott.

Who is this? and what is here?
And in the lighted palace near
Died the sound of royal cheer;
And they crossed themselves for fear,
    All the knights at Camelot:
But Lancelot mused a little space;
He said, 'She has a lovely face;
God in his mercy lend her grace,
    The Lady of Shalott.'

Alfred, Lord Tennyson
(1809–1892)

HELEN VENDLER
From *The Auroras of Autumn*, Wallace Stevens

Dear Students of Wesley College,
I am sorry to be answering you so late. I was in Japan for a month, and am only catching up.

My favorite poem is 'The Auroras of Autumn' by Wallace Stevens (1879–1955), our American great modernist poet. In it, Stevens confronts the exhaustion and destruction of everything we hold dear, and praises the sublimity of the human mind, which rises to meet and master, if only by imagination, the disasters of reality. This great hymn to change, even if change entails our own destruction, is Stevens's *summarium in excelsis*: 'Hear what he says, The dauntless master, as he starts the human tale.' This quotation, from Stevens's poem 'Puella Parvula', always comes to my mind when I re-read 'The Auroras of Autumn': it is the human tale of the innocent human being pitted against an impersonal but innocent necessitarian law of change.

Yours truly,
HELEN VENDLER
Professor of English

From *The Auroras of Autumn*

II

Farewell to an idea . . . A cabin stands,
Deserted, on a beach. It is white,
As by a custom or according to

An ancestral theme or as a consequence
Of an infinite course. The flowers against the wall
Are white, a little dried, a kind of mark

Reminding, trying to remind, of a white
That was different, something else, last year
Or before, not the white of an aging afternoon,

Whether fresher or duller, whether of winter cloud
Or of winter sky, from horizon to horizon.
The wind is blowing the sand across the floor.

Here, being visible is being white,
Is being of the solid of white, the accomplishment
Of an extremist in an exercise . . .

The season changes. A cold wind chills the beach.
The long lines of it grow longer, emptier,
A darkness gathers though it does not fall

And the whiteness grows less vivid on the wall.
The man who is walking turns blankly on the sand.
He observes how the north is always enlarging the
    change,

With its frigid brilliances, its blue-red sweeps
And gusts of great enkindlings, its polar green,
The color of ice and fire and solitude.

III

Farewell to an idea . . . The mother's face,
The purpose of the poem, fills the room.
They are together, here, and it is warm,

With none of the prescience of oncoming dreams,
It is evening. The house is evening, half dissolved.
Only the half they can never possess remains,

Still-starred. It is the mother they possess,
Who gives transparence to their present peace.
She makes that gentler that can gentle be.

And yet she too is dissolved, she is destroyed.
She gives transparence. But she has grown old.
The necklace is a carving not a kiss.

The soft hands are a motion not a touch.
The house will crumble and the books will burn.
They are at ease in a shelter of the mind

And the house is of the mind and they and time,
Together, all together. Boreal night
Will look like frost as it approaches them

And to the mother as she falls asleep
And as they say good-night, good-night. Upstairs
The windows will be lighted, not the rooms.

A wind will spread its windy grandeurs round
And knock like a rifle-butt against the door.
The wind will command them with invincible sound.

VII

Is there an imagination that sits enthroned
As grim as it is benevolent, the just
And the unjust, which in the midst of summer stops

To imagine winter? When the leaves are dead,
Does it take its place in the north and enfold itself,
Goat-leaper, crystalled and luminous, sitting

In highest night? And do these heavens adorn
And proclaim it, the white creator of black, jetted
By extinguishings, even of planets as may be,

Even of earth, even of sight, in snow,
Except as needed by way of majesty,
In the sky, as crown and diamond cabala?

It leaps through us, through all our heavens leaps,
Extinguishing our planets, one by one,
Leaving, of where we were and looked, of where

We knew each other and of each other thought,
A shivering residue, chilled and foregone,
Except for that crown and mystical cabala.

But it dare not leap by chance in its own dark.
It must change from destiny to slight caprice.
And thus its jetted tragedy, its stele

And shape and mournful making move to find
What must unmake it and, at last, what can,
Say, a flippant communication under the moon.

Wallace Stevens
(1879–1955)

NIAMH CUSACK
The Road Not Taken, Robert Frost

Dear Joann, Jacki and Carolyn,
I think these anthologies are a wonderful idea. Not only are they helping a very worthy cause but they're a grand old read. It's so interesting to learn of people's choices and their reasons for choosing certain poems.

I love poetry. I have crushes on different poets depending on my frame of mind. I think Shakespeare's sonnets are great for exercising your brain and plumbing the depths of human emotions and finding words and images that depict the grandeur of those emotions. All the sonnets I love. And Donne's. Yeats, Heaney, and Manley Hopkins are poets I dip into regularly. Oh yes, and Philip Larkin. There's a lovely collection by Wendy Cope called *Making Cocoa for Kingsley Amis*. But if I have to choose one poem it would be a very simple one called 'The Road Not Taken' by Robert Frost. I first read it when I was about thirteen and even then it struck a chord deep within me. First, I found it so lovely to speak and the image of the two roads in a yellow wood was clear for me to see. But it was the idea of choices changing your life for ever that has made this poem stick with me. At thirteen I wished myself a kindred spirit of Frost's when he wrote:

> Two roads diverged in a wood, and I –
> I took the one less traveled by,
> And that has made all the difference.

I hope I'm not too late for inclusion in *Lifelines*.

Good luck, and thank you for asking me.
NIAMH CUSACK

The Road Not Taken

Two roads diverged in a yellow wood,
And sorry I could not travel both
And be one traveler, long I stood
And looked down one as far as I could
To where it bent in the undergrowth;

Then took the other, as just as fair,
And having perhaps the better claim,
Because it was grassy and wanted wear;
Though as for that the passing there
Had worn them really about the same,

And both that morning equally lay
In leaves no step had trodden black.
Oh, I kept the first for another day!
Yet knowing how way leads on to way,
I doubted if I should ever come back.

I shall be telling this with a sigh
Somewhere ages and ages hence:
Two roads diverged in a wood, and I —
I took the one less traveled by,
And that has made all the difference.

Robert Frost
(1874–1963)

JOHN BAYLEY
Prologue to *Ruslan and Lyudmila*, Aleksandr Pushkin

My favourite poem is Pushkin's 'Ruslan and Lyudmila' because it is a wonderful fairy-story anyone can read and enjoy — in Russian or in translation — from the time they learn to read till the time they die.

Very best wishes to *Lifelines*.
JOHN BAYLEY

Пролог к «Руслану и Людмиле»

У лукоморья дуб зелёный;
Златая цепь на дубе том:
И днём и ночью кот учёный
Всё ходит по цепи кругом;
Идёт направо — песнь заводит,
Налево — сказку говорит.

Там чудеса: там леший бродит,
Русалка на ветвях сидит;
Там на неведомых дорожках

Следы невиданных зверей;
Избушка там на курьих ножках
Стоит без окон, без дверей;

Там лес и дол видений полны;
Там о заре прихлынут волны
На брег песчаный и пустой,
И тридцать витязей прекрасных
Чредой из вод выходят ясных,
И с ними дядька их морской;
Там королевич мимоходом
Пленяет грозного царя;
Там в облаках перед народом
Через леса, через моря
Колдун несёт богатыря;
В темнице там царевна тужит,
А бурый волк ей верно служит;
Там ступа с Вабою Ягой
Идёт, бредёт сама собой;
Там царь Кащей над златом чахнет;
Там русский дух ... там Русью пахнет!
И там я был, и мёд я пил;
У моря видел дуб зелёный;
Под ним сидел, и кот учёный
Свои мне сказки говорил.
Одну я помню: сказку эту
Поведаю теперь я свету ...

Aleksandr Pushkin
(1799–1837)

Prologue to *Ruslan and Lyudmila*

By the shores of a bay there is a green oak-tree; there is a golden chain on that oak; and day and night a learned cat ceaselessly walks round on the chain; as it moves to the right, it strikes up a song, as it moves to the left, it tells a story.

There are marvels there: the wood-sprite roams, a mermaid sits in the branches; there are tracks of strange animals on mysterious paths; a hut on hen's legs stands there, without windows or doors; forest and vale are full of visions; there at dawn the waves come washing over the sandy and deserted shore, and thirty fair knights come out one by one from the clear water, attended by their sea-tutor; a king's son, passing on his way, takes a dreaded king prisoner; there, in full view of the people, a sorcerer carries a knight through the clouds, across forests and seas; a princess pines away in prison, and a brown wolf serves her faithfully; a mortar with Baba-Yaga* in it walks along by itself. There King Kashchey† grows sickly beside his gold; there is a Russian odour there ... it smells of Russia! And I was there, I drank mead, I saw the green oak-tree by the sea and sat under it, while the learned cat told me its stories. I remember one – and this story I will now reveal to the world ...

* A wicked sorceress of Russian folk-tales.
† A rich and wicked old man of Russian folk-tales.

(Translated by John Bayley)

SUE TOWNSEND
'First they came for the Jews',
Pastor Niemöller

Dear Joann, Jacki and Carolyn,
My favourite poem is very short but, I think, powerful. I'm not even sure that it is a poem though it reads like poetry.

First they came for the Jews
and I did not speak out –
because I was not a Jew.
Then they came for the communists
and I did not speak out –
because I was not a communist.
Then they came for the trade unionists
and I did not speak out –
because I was not a trade unionist.
Then they came for me –
and there was no one left
to speak out for me.

Pastor Niemöller (victim of the Nazis)
(1892–1984)

I wish you all well in your fund-raising. All three of you obviously have
kind hearts – the very best thing to have.

Very best wishes,
SUE TOWNSEND

PETER FALLON
Hail Mary

To: The Editors of *Lifelines*
I don't know how I'd single out one poem as a favourite. So many verses are
central to my life as a writer, an editor, a reader. Still I appreciate opportunities
to attempt to direct people to patterns of words which I've come to love.
Perhaps, in this case, I am asking that familiar words be reconsidered, thought
about again. Thousands of times I've heard the 'Hail Mary' transformed into,
at best, a kind of mantra, at worst, the sound of no sense. Yet the words are
lovely in their pure praise of a woman, a mother – maybe all women – and the
phrase which has always delighted me, that is 'the fruit of thy womb', for an
offspring, a welcomed child, has again and again been submerged in the

interminable decades of a million galloping rosaries. One thoughtful recitation of this prayer would be worth those millions. Perhaps it's the editor in me which would propose to alter the order of the first section of the piece so that it ends 'Blessed is Jesus, the fruit of thy womb', to recover its special emphasis.

Now I'm no holy Joe but the plain beauty of this homage came to me first on my uncle's farm when I was a boy, when we congregated each evening and slumped as much as we were allowed on the arms of the drawing-room chairs and my brother Bernard (or BP if you like), on holidays from Prep School in England, knelt straight upright and spoke his pieces with the clear impression that he'd be a bishop at least, if not the Pope! Somehow the arch loveliness of the words and ideas filtered through to me then. I thought them perfectly married. I still do.

Thank you for asking me.

Very best wishes,
PETER FALLON

Hail Mary

Hail Mary, full of grace,
the Lord is with thee.
Blessed art thou amongst women
and blessed is the fruit of thy womb, Jesus.
Holy Mary, mother of God,
pray for us sinners,
now and at the hour of our death. Amen.

MOTHER TERESA
From *The New Testament*
Prayer for Peace, St Francis of Assisi

Dear Joann Bradish, Jacki Erskine and Carolyn Gibson,
Thank you for your letter of 1 January 1990. I am sure God is very pleased with your desire to serve the sick and save the lives of children through *Lifelines*. I feel nothing can be better than Christ's own words: 'Whatever

you do to the least of my brothers you do it to ME.' Jesus cannot deceive us – we can be sure that whatever we do for His poor, sick and suffering people, we do it for Him, and to Him. The same applies if we are unkind, uncharitable and unforgiving, we do it to Christ.

The Prayer for Peace of St Francis of Assisi is so beautiful and simple that we pray it daily after Mass. I would like to include it now. My prayer for you is that you may make this prayer your own and put it into your life and so become an instrument of Jesus's peace – the true peace that comes from loving and sharing and respecting everyone as a child of God – my Brother – my Sister.

I am praying for you and wish you a year of true Peace – that comes from loving and caring and from respecting the rights of every human being – even the unborn child.

God bless you,
MOTHER TERESA, MC

Prayer for Peace

Lord, make me a channel of Thy peace that where there is hatred, I may bring love; that where there is wrong, I may bring the spirit of forgiveness; that where there is discord, I may bring harmony; that where there is error, I may bring truth; that where there is doubt, I may bring faith; that where there is despair, I may bring hope; that where there are shadows, I may bring light; that where there is sadness, I may bring joy.

Lord, grant that I may seek rather to comfort than to be comforted; to understand than to be understood; to love than to be loved; for it is by forgetting self that one finds; it is by forgiving that one is forgiven; it is by dying that one awakens to eternal life.

Amen

St Francis of Assisi

ANTHONY CLARE
When You are Old, W. B. Yeats

I choose it because it never fails to move me when I read it, because it evokes the sweet, aching agony of nostalgia and ageing and the elusive, endlessly sought human love that every one of us seeks and because when I recite it myself I immediately feel my kinship, however slight, with the greatest poet in the English language in this century.

Best wishes,
ANTHONY W. CLARE

When You are Old

When you are old and grey and full of sleep,
And nodding by the fire, take down this book,
And slowly read, and dream of the soft look
Your eyes had once, and of their shadows deep;

How many loved your moments of glad grace,
And loved your beauty with love false or true,
But one man loved the pilgrim soul in you,
And loved the sorrows of your changing face;

And bending down beside the glowing bars,
Murmur, a little sadly, how Love fled
And paced upon the mountains overhead
And hid his face amid a crowd of stars.

W. B. Yeats
(1865–1939)

ANNA SCHER
Pied Beauty, Gerard Manley Hopkins

Dear Nicola, Paula and Alice,
Speaking as an Irish Jewish integrationist this poem really appeals to the warts-and-all in me as it celebrates individuality, its uniqueness and all the 'oddballness' that goes with it.

All the best with your excellent project,

Shalom for '92,
ANNA SCHER

Pied Beauty

Glory be to God for dappled things –
   For skies of couple-colour as a brinded cow;
     For rose-moles all in stipple upon trout that swim;
Fresh-firecoal chestnut-falls; finches' wings;
   Landscape plotted and pieced – fold, fallow, and plough;
And áll trádes, their gear and tackle and trim.

All things counter, original, spare, strange;
   Whatever is fickle, freckled (who knows how?)
     With swift, slow; sweet, sour; adazzle, dim;
He fathers-forth whose beauty is past change:
     Praise him.

Gerard Manley Hopkins
(1844–1889)

ROBIN EAMES
Psalm 121

Dear Editors,

Thank you for your recent letter. I would like to wish you every success in your venture. I am particularly pleased to know that the proceeds of the book will go to the Third World at this time when so many are suffering hunger and homelessness.

I have long regarded the Book of Psalms as one of the greatest collections of poetry in the world. While I enjoy poetry, I often find myself returning to the Psalms for the beauty of their language as much as their meaning. Psalm 121 holds particular interest for me:

> I will lift up mine eyes unto the hills,
> from whence cometh my help.

This language reminds me of the eternal strength of God and is reflected in the magnificent scenery we have in Ireland.

All good wishes,
ROBERT EAMES
Archbishop of Armagh and Primate of All Ireland

Psalm 121

I will lift up mine eyes unto the hills, from whence cometh my help. My help cometh from the Lord, which made heaven and earth. He will not suffer thy foot to be moved: he that keepeth thee will not slumber. Behold, he that keepeth Israel shall neither slumber nor sleep. The Lord is thy keeper; the Lord is thy shade upon thy right hand. The sun shall not smite thee by day, nor the moon by night. The Lord shall preserve thee from all evil; he shall preserve thy soul. The Lord shall preserve thy going out and thy coming in from this time forth, and even for evermore.

LYNN BARBER
Ozymandias, Percy Bysshe Shelley

Dear Nicola, Paula and Alice,

Thank you for your letter. Your *Lifelines* project sounds very worthwhile though I wish you had said exactly which Third World charities you support: as an atheist, I prefer not to be associated with any which have a religious basis.

My favourite poem is Shelley's 'Ozymandias' because it creates such an unforgettable picture of the ruined statue in the desert and quietly reminds us that all human pomp and power is transient and that even the greatest self-importance ends in dust. I love the commonplace, buttonholing way it opens, and then the grandeur of its climax. A few years ago I saw the ruined Pharaonic statue near Luxor which the poem is supposed to be based on: a bitter disappointment because it is beside a busy tourist road. But the glory of the poem remains.

Yours sincerely,
LYNN BARBER

Ozymandias

I met a traveller from an antique land
Who said – Two vast and trunkless legs of stone
Stand in the desert. Near them on the sand,
Half sunk a shatter'd visage lies, whose frown
And wrinkled lip and sneer of cold command
Tell that its sculptor well those passions read
Which yet survive, stamp'd on these lifeless things,
The hand that mock'd them, and the heart that fed;
And on the pedestal these words appear:
'My name is Ozymandias, king of kings:
Look on my works, ye Mighty, and despair!'
Nothing beside remains. Round the decay
Of that colossal wreck, boundless and bare,
The lone and level sands stretch far away.

Percy Bysshe Shelley
(1792–1822)

DORIS LESSING
Memory, W. B. Yeats

Dear Nicola Hughes, Paula Griffin and Alice McElency,
Yeats's poem 'Memory' has always been a favourite.

   This short and apparently simple poem has something of the quality of a
Japanese haiku – a great deal said in a few words, on whatever level it is
being understood.

With good wishes,
DORIS LESSING

Memory

One had a lovely face,
And two or three had charm,
But charm and face were in vain
Because the mountain grass
Cannot but keep the form
Where the mountain hare has lain.

W. B. Yeats
(1865–1939)

Y COOPER
n *The Rime of the Ancient Mariner*,
nuel Taylor Coleridge

Thank you for your lovely letter.

I'm very proud to be asked to be part of *Lifelines* and I enclose a copy of my favourite poem, which is an extract from *The Ancient Mariner*. It's obviously far too long a poem for you to publish the whole thing, but I just think that this bit is particularly beautiful because it tells people that the only thing that really matters in life is to be kind and only if we can be kind to the smallest creatures will we learn to be kind to each other. I think it's a very beautiful poem and still when I read it, it makes the hair prickle on the back of my neck. I hope you like it too.

Lots of love,
JILLY COOPER

From *The Rime of the Ancient Mariner*

PART IV

Beyond the shadow of the ship,
I watched the water snakes:
They moved in tracks of shining white,
And when they reared, the elfish light
Fell off in hoary flakes.

Within the shadow of the ship
I watched their rich attire:
Blue, glossy green, and velvet black,
They coiled and swam; and every track
Was a flash of golden fire.

O happy living things! no tongue
Their beauty might declare:
A spring of love gushed from my heart,

And I blessed them unaware:
Sure my kind saint took pity on me,
And I blessed them unaware.

The selfsame moment I could pray;
And from my neck so free
The Albatross fell off, and sank
Like lead into the sea.

> Samuel Taylor Coleridge
> (1772–1834)

SHANE CONNAUGHTON
Quote from Muhammad Ali

Girls,
My favourite poem has no name and only one line and isn't normally thought of as poetry at all.

> I ain't got no quarrel with them Vietcong.

It was spoken by Muhammad Ali, the greatest boxer and sportsman this century. He said it to the US Government when refusing to join the army to fight in Vietnam.

The line comes from the heart where all poetry comes from and has a real beat to it when you recite it aloud. It is pure rap. Rap is the street poetry of Black America. 'I ain't got no quarrel with them Vietcong.' It has music and truth. He stood against the Establishment like Byron, Shelley and Blake before him. And he was proven right! By saying that line he risked all. How many poets today can say the same?

Good luck to you all.

Sincerely,
SHANE CONNAUGHTON

V. S. PRITCHETT
From *Amours de Voyage*,
Arthur Hugh Clough

One of my favourite poets is Arthur Hugh Clough – *Amours de Voyage*. It delights me. His dates are 1819–1861. I love its appeal to courage and its autobiographical tone.

V. S. PRITCHETT

From *Amours de Voyage*
Canto I

I – CLAUDE TO EUSTACE

Dear Eustatio, I write that you may write me an answer,
Or at the least to put us again *en rapport* with each other.
Rome disappoints me much, – St Peter's, perhaps, in
    especial;
Only the Arch of Titus and view from the Lateran please
    me:
This, however, perhaps is the weather, which truly is
    horrid.
Greece must be better, surely; and yet I am feeling so
    spiteful
That I could travel to Athens, to Delphi, and Troy, and
    Mount Sinai,
Though but to see with my eyes that these are vanity also.
    Rome disappoints me much; I hardly as yet understand,
      but
Rubbishy seems the word that most exactly would suit it.
All the foolish destructions, and all the sillier savings,
All the incongruous things of past incompatible ages,
Seem to be treasured up here to make fools of present and
    future.

Would to Heaven the old Goths had made a cleaner sweep
   of it!
Would to Heaven some new ones would come and destroy
   these churches!
However, one can live in Rome as also in London.
It is a blessing, no doubt, to be rid, at least for a time, of
All one's friends and relations, – yourself (forgive me!)
   included, –
All the *assujettissement* of having been what one has been,
What one thinks one is, or thinks that others suppose one;
Yet, in despite of all, we turn like fools to the English.
Vernon has been my fate; who is here the same that you
   knew him, –
Making the tour, it seems, with friends of the name of
   Trevellyn.

                                        Arthur Hugh Clough
                                        (1819–1861)

FERDIA MAC ANNA
Buying Winkles, Paula Meehan

Dear Paula,
My favourite poem of the moment is 'Buying Winkles' from Paula
Meehan's collection *The Man Who was Marked by Winter*. I like it because
it is direct, simple and beautiful, and because it conjures up images of a
child's experience of the adult world. Each time I read it, I find something
new to savour. Most of all though, I like this poem because of its strong
cinematic flavour. Reading it is a bit like being inside an imaginary Fellini
film set in Dublin – there is colour, dash, charm, light and character as well
as an ever-present tinge of danger.

   I love this kind of work. I think it gives Poetry a good name. Also, I
think Paula Meehan is a great writer.

   I hope all the above is helpful. Good luck with the project.

                                        Regards,
                                        FERDIA MAC ANNA

Buying Winkles

My mother would spare me sixpence and say,
'Hurry up now and don't be talking to strange
men on the way.' I'd dash from the ghosts
on the stairs where the bulb had blown
out into Gardiner Street, all relief.
A bonus if the moon was in the strip of sky
between the tall houses, or stars out,
but even in rain I was happy – the winkles
would be wet and glisten blue like little
night skies themselves. I'd hold the tanner tight
and jump every crack in the pavement,
I'd wave up to women at sills or those
lingering in doorways and weave a glad path through
men heading out for the night.

She'd be sitting outside the Rosebowl Bar
on an orange-crate, a pram loaded
with pails of winkles before her.
When the bar doors swung open they'd leak
the smell of men together with drink
and I'd see light in golden mirrors.
I envied each soul in the hot interior.

I'd ask her again to show me the right way
to do *it*. She'd take a pin from her shawl –
'Open the eyelid. So. Stick it in
till you feel a grip, then slither him out.
Gently, mind.' The sweetest extra winkle
that brought the sea to me.
'Tell yer Ma I picked them fresh this morning.'

I'd bear the newspaper twists
bulging fat with winkles
proudly home, like torches.

Paula Meehan
(b. 1955)

SIMON ARMITAGE
The More Loving One, W. H. Auden

Dear Nicola, Paula and Alice,
Many thanks for your invitation. Good luck with the project.

'The More Loving One' by W. H. Auden (1907–1973). Favourite poems come and go, and although I wouldn't claim that this is the greatest piece ever written, it has stayed with me longer than most. On the face of it I'm attracted to its casual but compelling tone, its shifting rhythms and acoustics, its brevity, as well as its sentiments, which I can more or less subscribe to. The second stanza is exceptional – my heart goes off like a flash-bulb every time I read it. More than this, whilst the poem would be at home in any anthology of modern verse, it would be equally as comfortable on a toilet door or the back of a bus seat, and none the worse for it.

Very best,
SIMON ARMITAGE

The More Loving One

Looking up at the stars, I know quite well
That, for all they care, I can go to hell.
But on earth indifference is the least
We have to dread from man or beast.

How should we like it were stars to burn
With a passion for us we could not return?
If equal affection cannot be,
Let the more loving one be me.

Admirer as I think I am
Of stars that do not give a damn,
I cannot, now I see them, say
I missed one terribly all day.

Were all stars to disappear or die
I should learn to look at an empty sky
And feel its total dark sublime,
Though this might take me a little time.

W. H. Auden
(1907–1973)

JOSEPH O'CONNOR
Happiness, Raymond Carver

Dear Nicola, Paula, Alice,
Thanks very much for your recent note about the *Lifelines IV* book. It sounds like a good idea, and I'm happy to be involved.

I don't really have one favourite poem but I like Raymond Carver's 'Happiness' a lot. I like the clarity of it. It's lucid and atmospheric and very moving. For me, what makes a poem work is the sense that it *had* to be written. Carver's poems and short stories are alive with that quality.

Warmest best wishes,
JOSEPH O'CONNOR

Happiness

So early it's still almost dark out.
I'm near the window with coffee,
and the usual early morning stuff
that passes for thought.
When I see the boy and his friend
walking up the road
to deliver the newspaper.
They wear caps and sweaters,

and one boy has a bag over his shoulder.
They are so happy
they aren't saying anything, these boys.
I think if they could, they would take
each other's arm.
It's early in the morning,
and they are doing this thing together.
They come on, slowly.
The sky is taking on light,
though the moon still hangs pale over the water.
Such beauty that for a minute
death and ambition, even love,
doesn't enter into this.
Happiness. It comes on
unexpectedly. And goes beyond, really,
any early morning talk about it.

Raymond Carver
(1938–1988)

ANNE FINE
Summer Song I, George Barker
A Slice of Wedding Cake,
Robert Graves

Dear Nicola, Paula and Alice,
I'm delighted to be part of *Lifelines*, because I was so impressed with the
two I have, and you all work on it for such good reasons. I've given up
trying to choose a *favourite* poem. Here's George Barker's 'Summer Song I',
which I'm not sure I understand, but the last three verses haunted me all
through my late childhood, and after. And 'A Slice of Wedding Cake', by

Robert Graves. I really don't know why I like it so much, except that Graves is one of my favourite poets, and this one should amuse people your age!

All good wishes,
Yours sincerely,
ANNE FINE

Summer Song I

I looked into my heart to write
    And found a desert there.
But when I looked again I heard
Howling and proud in every word
    The hyena despair.

Great summer sun, great summer sun,
    All loss burns in trophies;
And in the cold sheet of the sky
Lifelong the fish-lipped lovers lie
    Kissing catastrophes.

O loving garden where I lay
    When under the breasted tree
My son stood up behind my eyes
And groaned: Remember that the price
    Is vinegar for me.

Great summer sun, great summer sun,
    Turn back to the designer:
I would not be the one to start
The breaking day and the breaking heart
    For all the grief in China.

My one, my one, my only love,
    Hide, hide your face in a leaf,
And let the hot tear falling burn
The stupid heart that will not learn
    The everywhere of grief.

Great summer sun, great summer sun,
    Turn back to the never-never
Cloud-cuckoo, happy, far-off land
Where all the love is true love, and
    True love goes on for ever.

              George Barker
              (1913–1991)

A Slice of Wedding Cake

Why have such scores of lovely, gifted girls
    Married impossible men?
Simple self-sacrifice may be ruled out,
    And missionary endeavour, nine times out of ten.

Repeat 'impossible men'; not merely rustic,
    Foul-tempered or depraved
(Dramatic foils chosen to show the world
    How well women behave, and always have behaved).

Impossible men: idle, illiterate,
    Self-pitying, dirty, sly,
For whose appearance even in City parks
    Excuses must be made to casual passers-by.

Has God's supply of tolerable husbands
    Fallen, in fact, so low?
Or do I always over-value woman
    At the expense of man?
              Do I?
                  It might be so.

              Robert Graves
              (1895–1985)

CHRISTY MOORE
Cuckoo, Seán Lysaght

Dear Nicola, Paula and Alice,
My father Christy Moore asked me to write, sending the poem 'Cuckoo'
by Seán Lysaght in reply to your letter.

Yours sincerely,
JAMES MOORE

PS. I think it would be fitting if you could include the title of the collection
from which this poem I read, also the publishers, thus allowing your
readers the opportunity to read some more.

Sincerely,
CHRISTY

Cuckoo

Scarcer now
than when he named himself
to every meadow in the townland
when the hay was down,

as I stood on the butt of the wain,
bedding in what tumbled from the pikes
with *cuck-oo*
repeated from the next acre.

So I drifted off
to stalk nearer the bird.
The song got louder
along the bristly edge of the headland.

I hadn't said a word
when my uncle came
calling 'Seán!'
and so I lost the cuckoo.

Seán Lysaght
(b. 1957)
(From *The Clare Island Survey*, The Gallery Press, 1991)

GLENDA JACKSON
Not Waving but Drowning, Stevie Smith

Dear Nicola, Paula and Alice,
Thank you for your letter.
   I don't really have a favourite poem, but I would choose 'Not Waving
but Drowning' by Stevie Smith, because I share her feeling.
   Best wishes for your book and I hope it will raise a wonderful sum of money.

Yours sincerely,
GLENDA JACKSON

Not Waving but Drowning

Nobody heard him, the dead man,
But still he lay moaning:
I was much further out than you thought
And not waving but drowning.

Poor chap, he always loved larking
And now he's dead
It must have been too cold for him his heart gave way,
They said.

Oh, no no no, it was too cold always
(Still the dead one lay moaning)
I was much too far out all my life
And not waving but drowning.

Stevie Smith
(1902–1971)

JULIAN BARNES
Last Poems, XII, A. E. Housman

Dear Nicola Hughes, Paula Griffin and Alice McEleney,
Thank you for your letter about *Lifelines IV*. I am enclosing one of my
favourite poems, by A. E. Housman, with a few lines about it. Good luck
with your project.

Yours sincerely,
JULIAN BARNES

This untitled poem, number XII from Housman's *Last Poems*, was written
in circa 1900, and could have been addressed to our whole century. It is a
passionate plea for individualism, for the right to be oneself, against the
bullyings of religion and one's fellow men, against those who are sure they
know all the answers. It uses simple words, and is in simple couplets, but is
far from being a cool, 'argument' poem: listen for the rage, the protest, the
hurt, the stoicism. Listen, in particular, to the implications of that sly phrase
in the penultimate line, 'if keep we can'.

Last Poems

XII

The laws of God, the laws of man,
He may keep that will and can;
Not I: let God and man decree

Laws for themselves and not for me;
And if my ways are not as theirs
Let them mind their own affairs.
Their deeds I judge and much condemn,
Yet when did I make laws for them?
Please yourselves, say I, and they
Need only look the other way.
But no, they will not; they must still
Wrest their neighbour to their will,
And make me dance as they desire
With jail and gallows and hell-fire.
And how am I to face the odds
Of man's bedevilment and God's?
I, a stranger and afraid
In a world I never made.
They will be master, right or wrong;
Though both are foolish, both are strong.
And since, my soul, we cannot fly
To Saturn nor to Mercury,
Keep we must, if keep we can,
These foreign laws of God and man.

A. E. Housman
(1859–1936)

CHRISTOPHER RICKS
To E. FitzGerald,
Alfred, Lord Tennyson

Dear Nicola Hughes, Paula Griffin and Alice McElency,
Sorry about the delay; have been away. (Poet but he doesn't know it.)
Lifelines: A good thing about the word 'favourite' (my favourite poem) is
that it doesn't have to be the same as the poem you think the *best*. So:

Alfred Tennyson, 'To E. FitzGerald' (note the capital G in the middle . . .).
A lovely poem from a great poet to a true poet, the translator of the
Rubaiyat of Omar Khayyam; an act of friendship, over the years (they had
been college friends, and are now in their seventies); no condescension
(Tennyson the *Poet Laureate*, for Victoria's sake): one sentence rippling
through fifty-six lines, but never unravelling; and coming to rest with the
word 'praise' – which it so deserves itself.

Best wishes,
CHRISTOPHER RICKS

To E. FitzGerald

Old Fitz, who from your suburb grange,
    Where once I tarried for a while,
Glance at the wheeling Orb of change,
    And greet it with a kindly smile;
Whom yet I see as there you sit
    Beneath your sheltering garden-tree,
And while your doves about you flit,
    And plant on shoulder, hand and knee,
Or on your head their rosy feet,
    As if they knew your diet spares
Whatever moved in that full sheet
    Let down to Peter at his prayers;
Who live on milk and meal and grass;
    And once for ten long weeks I tried
Your table of Pythagoras,
    And seemed at first 'a thing enskied'
(As Shakespeare has it) airy-light
    To float above the ways of men,
Then fell from that half-spiritual height
    Chilled, till I tasted flesh again
One night when earth was winter-black,
    And all the heavens flashed in frost;
And on me, half-asleep, came back
    That wholesome heat the blood had lost,

And set me climbing icy capes
   And glaciers, over which there rolled
To meet me long-armed vines with grapes
   Of Eshcol hugeness; for the cold
Without, and warmth within me, wrought
   To mould the dream; but none can say
That Lenten fare makes Lenten thought,
   Who reads your golden Eastern lay,
Than which I know no version done
   In English more divinely well;
A planet equal to the sun
   Which cast it, that large infidel
Your Omar; and your Omar drew
   Full-handed plaudits from our best
In modern letters, and from two,
   Old friends outvaluing all the rest,
Two voices heard on earth no more;
   But we old friends are still alive,
And I am nearing seventy-four,
   While you have touched at seventy-five,
And so I send a birthday line
   Of greeting; and my son, who dipt
In some forgotten book of mine
   With sallow scraps of manuscript,
And dating many a year ago,
   Has hit on this, which you will take
My Fitz, and welcome, as I know
   Less for its own than for the sake
Of one recalling gracious times,
   When, in our younger London days,
You found some merit in my rhymes,
   And I more pleasure in your praise.

               Alfred, Lord Tennyson
               (1809–1892)

KENNETH BRANAGH
Fear No More the Heat o' the Sun,
William Shakespeare

Dear Nicola Hughes, Paula Griffin and Alice McEleney,
Thank you for your letter to Kenneth Branagh.

His favourite poem/song is 'Fear No More the Heat o' the Sun' from Shakespeare's *Cymbeline*.

He feels it is the most moving and beautiful commentary on life and death. Simple and profound.

Wishing you every success with *Lifelines*.

Yours sincerely,
TAMAR THOMAS
Assistant to Mr Branagh

Fear No More the Heat o' the Sun

Fear no more the heat o' the sun,
    Nor the furious winter's rages;
Thou thy worldly task hast done,
    Home art gone, and ta'en thy wages;
Golden lads and girls all must
    As chimney-sweepers, come to dust.

Fear no more the frown o' the great,
    Thou art past the tyrant's stroke:
Care no more to clothe and eat;
    To thee the reed is as the oak;
The sceptre, learning, physic, must
    All follow this, and come to dust.

Fear no more the lightning-flash,
    Nor the all-dreaded thunder-stone;
Fear not slander, censure rash;
    Thou hast finish'd joy and moan:

All lovers young, all lovers must
　　Consign to thee, and come to dust.

No exorcizer harm thee!
　　Nor no witchcraft charm thee!
Ghost unlaid forbear thee!
　　Nothing ill come near thee!
Quiet consummation have;
　　And renowned be thy grave!

William Shakespeare
(1564–1616)

ANTHONY CRONIN
Whenever I Think of Francis,
Anne Haverty

Dear Editors,
I never know what my favourite poem of all is because there are so many
and I am constantly being bowled over by new discoveries.

My favourite poem of the moment is a poem about the great Irish
writer, Francis Stuart, by Anne Haverty. It will, I believe, be published in a
Canadian university publication in celebration of Francis's ninetieth birth-
day. You may find it difficult to get a copy of the magazine so I am
enclosing a typescript copy of the poem.

Anne Haverty's 'Whenever I Think of Francis' is a lovely poem about a
great writer which manages to do honour to its subject while being very
tender, personal and moving at the same time.

Yours sincerely,
ANTHONY CRONIN

Whenever I Think of Francis

Whenever I think of Francis
Stuart I think of Easter.
In a warm wind blowing from the west
he is going with his mediaeval monk's
face to feed a young goat
leaping on the rock.
Actually he is walking in the direction
of Nassau Street when the October
evening is drawing in but
it seems the light glows longer
than it did yesterday and
flowers in the far North that were
dying out during the afternoon
are beginning to bloom again.
For the last of the great
Christian festivals left to us
uncolonised by commerce, we are
preparing a frugal and sweet repast,
almonds, chocolate and spring lamb.
Whenever I think of Francis
limping like a boy
who fell out of a tree,
I think of the feast of Resurrection.

Anne Haverty

THOMAS DOCHERTY
Crazy Weather, John Ashbery

Dear Nicola, Paula, Alice,

Very many thanks for your most kind invitation to select a poem for inclusion in *Lifelines IV*. Living surrounded by poetry, as I do, makes it difficult to select a single favourite. Others – those to whom the volume is dedicated – have to live surrounded by poverty and injustice; their difficulties are much greater. It would be easy for me to choose a poem with some obvious political point, but in this instance I would prefer to propose a text which is not in any sense directly political. John Ashbery's 'Crazy Weather' is, like all his writing, difficult and obscure. My sense when I read it is that I am somehow reading a poem in a foreign language: it makes the world I thought I knew seem less sure, less clear, less known. Like all the best poetry, it deploys its own art, its aesthetic, to produce a shift in the everyday world, the political world; like all the best writing, it offers a second world, adjacent to, but different from, our own. May it also give something to a Third World.

With very best wishes for the success of the volume.

Yours sincerely,
THOMAS DOCHERTY

Crazy Weather

It's this crazy weather we've been having:
Falling forward one minute, lying down the next
Among the loose grasses and soft, white, nameless flowers.
People have been making a garment out of it,
Stitching the white of lilacs together with lightning
At some anonymous crossroads. The sky calls
To the deaf earth. The proverbial disarray
Of morning corrects itself as you stand up.
You are wearing a text. The lines
Droop to your shoelaces and I shall never want or need
Any other literature than this poetry of mud
And ambitious reminiscences of times when it came easily

Through the then woods and ploughed fields and had
A simple unconscious dignity we can never hope to
Approximate now except in narrow ravines nobody
Will inspect where some late sample of the rare,
Uninteresting specimen might still be putting out shoots,
    for all we know.

John Ashbery
(b. 1927)

MICHAEL LONGLEY
From *Voyages*, Hart Crane

I hope the enclosed will be of some use to you.

'Voyages' (II) by Hart Crane

A favourite poem is not necessarily the best poem by a poet whom one admires more than all – or even most – other poets. For me it is a piece which took me completely by surprise once, and continues to do so without my ever being able to comprehend its 'meaning' or follow its processes. A spell has been cast. 'Fern Hill' by Dylan Thomas; Yeats's 'Byzantium'; 'Tall Nettles' by Edward Thomas; 'Innocence' by Patrick Kavanagh; 'Mayfly' by Louis MacNeice; D. H. Lawrence's 'Bavarian Gentians' are all candidates for the dubious privilege of being My Favourite Poem. (And I have confined myself to this century.)

I choose 'Voyages' (II) by the American poet Hart Crane. It is the high point of a sequence of lyrics, each one a great psalm to the sea. Sensuous yet spiritual, unabashed in its erotic embrace, unembarrassed by its own over-reaching rhetoric, Crane's incantation risks failing ludicrously. Instead, here is a poem which has everything. After hundreds of readings it remains for me a revelation. When Hart Crane wrote at this altitude his genius became a small part of the universe, one of its wonders.

Best wishes,
MICHAEL LONGLEY

P.S. My favourite *line* of poetry is the last line of 'Voyages' (III): 'Permit me voyage, love, into your hands . . .'

Voyages

II

– And yet this great wink of eternity,
Of rimless floods, unfettered leewardings,
Samite sheeted and processioned where
Her undinal vast belly moonward bends,
Laughing the wrapt inflections of our love;

Take this Sea, whose diapason knells
On scrolls of silver snowy sentences,
The sceptred terror of whose sessions rends
As her demeanors motion well or ill,
All but the pieties of lovers' hands.

And onward, as bells off San Salvador
Salute the crocus lustres of the stars,
In these poinsettia meadows of her tides, –
Adagios of islands, O my Prodigal,
Complete the dark confessions her veins spell.

Mark how her turning shoulders wind the hours,
And hasten while her penniless rich palms
Pass superscription of bent foam and wave, –
Hasten, while they are true, – sleep, death, desire,
Close round one instant in one floating flower.

Bind us in time, O Seasons clear, and awe.
O minstrel galleons of Carib fire,
Bequeath us to no earthly shore until
Is answered in the vortex of our grave
The seal's wide spindrift gaze toward paradise.

Hart Crane
(1899–1932)

RICHARD MURPHY
Bread, Boris Pasternak

Dear Nicola, Paula and Alice,
Thank you for your New Year's Day letter about your anthology. I hope it will be successful.

I enclose my contribution: a poem by Pasternak called 'Bread' in an English version by Michael Harari, followed by my comments.

Bread

With half a century to pile,
    Unwritten, your conclusions,
    By now, if you're not a halfwit,
You should have lost a few illusions,

    Grasped the pleasure of study,
The laws and secrets of success,
The curse of idleness, the heroism
    Needed for happiness;

    That the powerful kingdom of beasts,
The sleepy kingdom of vegetation
    Await their heroes, giants,
Their altars and their revelation;

That first of all the revelations,
    Father of living and dead,
Gift to the generations, growth
    Of the centuries, is bread;

And a harvest field is not just wheat
    But a page to understand,
    Written about yourself
In your remote forefather's hand,

His very word, his own amazing
Initiative among the birth,
    Sorrow and death that circle
    Their set ways round the earth.

Boris Pasternak
(1890–1960)
(Translated by Michael Harari)

Boris Pasternak's poem 'Bread' in the English version by Michael Harari
has been a favourite poem of mine since a friend showed it to me about
fifteen years ago. It was then a purifying antidote to the toxic effects of
creative writing at Iowa during the coldest winter on record. It still seems
to have a mysterious power to say everything under the sun in a way that
sounds new. I can't imagine what gets lost in this translation, apart from
rhyme, because the poetry comes through with visionary force.

If that sounds grandiloquent, it's because I think Pasternak has taken a
high risk in daring to make a conclusive comment on what life seems to
him to be all about. Wisely he uses the admonishing tone of voice of an
alter ego or a conscience or the muse. He addresses himself as 'you': and
you as a reader feel yourself drawn inside his thought process, becoming
transformed into a better person as you read.

The great metaphor of the harvest field, as 'a page to understand, written
about yourself in your remote forefather's hand' is, at least, an original way
of seeing the link between the discovery of agriculture and the invention of
writing. The biblical word 'forefather' may suggest God, but at earth level
it projects our unknown primitive ancestors, perhaps in the valleys of the
Jordan and the Euphrates, whose 'amazing initiative' began the process that
has enabled us to probe beyond the furthest visible stars.

The word 'forefather', like 'mankind', may disturb readers affected by
the feminist assault on sexist vocabulary. Since seed was cast in a fenced
field, and bread baked, women have done much of the work, while men
have been waging war. I don't think Pasternak, or his translator, intended
the word 'forefather' to exclude the idea of motherhood, but to be
inclusive. If he'd used a neuter word, such as 'originator', humanity would
have been drained out of his poem at its climax. Instead, without losing
his foothold on the ground, he rises to a new affirmation of the mythical
link between bread and the word, or logos. To express the search through
the self and the cosmos for salvation, he uses a tone of voice unflawed by
religiosity.

Before he works this beneficial magic, he rings bells as common as those
that chime from village or city clock towers. If the clichés in the first two

stanzas sound banal, their banality is soon transmuted into the poem's myth. And the bread is revealed as the truth. Pasternak had suffered through the famine caused by Stalin's policy of collectivization, the terror under Stalin, and the horrors of war. He had earned the moral authority with which he speaks of 'the heroism needed for happiness'.

'Bread' was written in the mid fifties. Bearing this in mind while reading the final stanza, I recall the first sputnik moving across the sky before dawn over Dublin, where I watched it from the cattle-markets. Russia was then winning the space race by an 'amazing initiative', putting a dog into orbit. The unfortunate creature received a lethal injection when its job of contributing to a triumph of human technology was finished. In a sense that is literal and shocking, the dog on its doomed voyage underscores and confirms Pasternak's final metaphor of the 'birth, sorrow and death that circle their set ways round the earth'. The poem has become all the more relevant in the winter of 1991/2, when a great number of desperate people in Russia and the Third World cannot obtain enough bread.

With best wishes,
RICHARD MURPHY

CONOR CRUISE O'BRIEN
Ode *On the Morning of Christ's Nativity*, John Milton

Dear Nicola, Paula and Alice
Here goes:
My favourite poem is Milton's Ode 'On the Morning of Christ's Nativity', which I usually read aloud to my family on Christmas Day. I love the poem mainly because of the splendour of the language and imagery and my love of all that is tinged with incredulous horror, both at Christian redemption theology in itself and also at the association of that theology with baroque grandeur.

Best wishes for the New Year.

Yours sincerely,
CONOR CRUISE O'BRIEN

On the Morning of Christ's Nativity

I

This is the Month, and this the happy morn
Wherein the Son of Heav'ns eternal King,
Of wedded Maid, and Virgin Mother born,
Our great redemption from above did bring
For so the holy sages once did sing,
 That he our deadly forfeit should release,
And with his Father work us a perpetual peace.

II

That glorious Form, that Light unsufferable,
And that far-beaming blaze of Majesty,
Wherwith he wont at Heav'ns high Councel-Table,
To sit the midst of Trinal Unity,
He laid aside; and here with us to be,
 Forsook the Courts of everlasting Day,
And chose with us a darksom House of mortal Clay.

III

Say Heav'nly Muse, shall not thy sacred vein
Afford a present to the Infant God?
Hast thou no vers, no hymn, or solemn strein,
To welcom him to this his new abode,
Now while the Heav'n by the Suns team untrod,
 Hath took no print of the approaching light,
And all the spangled host keep watch in squadrons bright?

IV

See how from far upon the Eastern rode
The Star-led Wisards haste with odours sweet,
O run, prevent them with thy humble ode,
And lay it lowly at his blessed feet;
Have thou the honour first, thy Lord to greet,
 And joyn thy voice unto the Angel Quire,
From out his secret Altar toucht with hallow'd fire.

The Hymn

I

It was the Winter wilde,
While the Heav'n-born-childe,
    All meanly wrapt in the rude manger lies;
Nature in aw to him
Had doff't her gawdy trim,
    With her great Master so to sympathize:
It was no season then for her
To wanton with the Sun her lusty Paramour.

II

Only with speeches fair
She woo's the gentle Air
    To hide her guilty front with innocent Snow,
And on her naked shame,
Pollute with sinfull blame,
    The Saintly Vail of Maiden white to throw,
Confounded, that her Makers eyes
Should look so neer upon her foul deformities.

III

But he her fears to cease,
Sent down the meek-eyd Peace,
    She crown'd with Olive green, came softly sliding
Down through the turning sphear
His ready Harbinger,
    With Turtle wing the amorous clouds dividing,
And waving wide her mirtle wand,
She strikes a universall Peace through Sea and Land.

IV

No War, or Battails sound
Was heard the World around,
    The idle spear and shield were high up hung;
The hooked Chariot stood
Unstain'd with hostile blood,
    The Trumpet spake not to the armed throng,
And Kings sate still with awfull eye,
As if they surely knew their sovran Lord was by.

V

But peacefull was the night
Wherin the Prince of light
   His raign of peace upon the earth began:
The Windes with wonder whist,
Smoothly the waters kist,
    Whispering new joyes to the milde Ocean,
Who now hath quite forgot to rave,
While Birds of Calm sit brooding on the charmed wave.

VI

The Stars with deep amaze
Stand fixt in steadfast gaze,
   Bending one way their pretious influence,
And will not take their flight,
For all the morning light,
   Or *Lucifer* that often warn'd them thence;
But in their glimmering Orbs did glow,
Untill their Lord himself bespake, and bid them go.

VII

And though the shady gloom
Had given day her room,
   The Sun himself with-held his wonted speed,
And hid his head for shame,
As his inferiour flame,
   The New enlightn'd world no more should need;
He saw a greater Sun appear
Then his bright Throne, or burning Axletree could bear.

VIII

The Shepherds on the Lawn,
Or ere the point of dawn,
   Sate simply chatting in a rustick row;
Full little thought they than,
That the mighty *Pan*
   Was kindly com to live with them below;
Perhaps their loves, or els their sheep,
Was all that did their silly thoughts so busie keep.

IX

When such musick sweet
Their hearts and ears did greet,
   As never was by mortall finger strook,
Divinely-warbled voice
Answering the stringed noise,
   As all their souls in blisfull rapture took:
The Air such pleasure loth to lose,
With thousand echo's still prolongs each heav'nly close.

X

Nature that heard such sound
Beneath the hollow round
   Of *Cynthia*'s seat, the Airy region thrilling,
Now was almost won
To think her part was don,
   And that her raign had here its last fulfilling;
She knew such harmony alone
Could hold all Heav'n and Earth in happier union.

XI

At last surrounds their sight
A Globe of circular light,
   That with long beams the shame-fac't night array'd,
The helmed Cherubim
And sworded Seraphim,
   Are seen in glittering ranks with wings displaid,
Harping in loud and solemn quire,
With unexpressive notes to Heav'ns new-born Heir.

XII

Such Musick (as 'tis said)
Before was never made,
   But when of old the sons of morning sung,
While the Creator Great
His constellations set,
   And the well-ballanc't world on hinges hung,
And cast the dark foundations deep,
And bid the weltring waves their oozy channel keep.

XIII

Ring out ye Crystall sphears,
Once bless our human ears,
   (If ye have power to touch our senses so)
And let your silver chime
Move in melodious time;
   And let the Base of Heav'ns deep Organ blow,
And with your ninefold harmony
Make up full consort to th'Angelike symphony.

XIV

For if such holy Song
Enwrap our fancy long,
   Time will run back, and fetch the age of gold,
And speckl'd vanity
Will sicken soon and die,
   And leprous sin will melt from earthly mould,
And Hell it self will pass away,
And leave her dolorous mansions to the peering day.

XV

Yea Truth, and Justice then
Will down return to men,
   Orb'd in a Rain-bow; and like glories wearing
Mercy will sit between,
Thron'd in Celestiall sheen,
   With radiant feet the tissued clouds down stearing,
And Heav'n as at som festivall,
Will open wide the Gates of her high Palace Hall.

XVI

But wisest Fate sayes no,
This must not yet be so,
   The Babe lies yet in smiling Infancy,
That on the bitter cross
Must redeem our loss;
   So both himself and us to glorifie:
Yet first to those ychain'd in sleep,
The wakefull trump of doom must thunder through the
   deep.

XVII

With such a horrid clang
As on mount *Sinai* rang
   While the red fire, and smouldring clouds out brake:
The aged Earth agast
With terrour of that blast,
   Shall from the surface to the center shake;
When at the worlds last session,
The dreadfull Judge in middle Air shall spread his throne.

XVIII

And then at last our bliss
Full and perfect is,
   But now begins; far from this happy day
Th'old Dragon under ground
In straiter limits bound,
   Not half so far casts his usurped sway,
And wrath to see his Kingdom fail,
Swindges the scaly Horrour of his foulded tail.

XIX

The Oracles are dumm,
No voice or hideous humm
   Runs through the arched roof in words deceiving.
Apollo from his shrine
Can no more divine,
   With hollow shreik the steep of *Delphos* leaving.
No nightly trance, or breathed spell,
Inspire's the pale-ey'd Priest from the prophetic cell.

XX

The lonely mountains o're,
And the resounding shore,
   A voice of weeping heard, and loud lament;
From haunted spring, and dale
Edg'd with poplar pale,
   The parting Genius is with sighing sent,
With flowre-inwov'n tresses torn
The Nimphs in twilight shade of tangled thickets mourn.

XXI

In consecrated Earth,
And on the holy Hearth,
   The *Lars*, and *Lemures* moan with midnight plaint,
In Urns, and Altars round,
A drear, and dying sound
   Affrights the *Flamins* at their service quaint;
And the chill Marble seems to sweat,
While each peculiar power forgoes his wonted seat.

XXII

Peor, and *Baalim*
Forsake their Temples dim,
   With that twise-batter'd god of *Palestine*,
And mooned *Ashtaroth*,
Heav'ns Queen and Mother both,
   Now sits not girt with Tapers holy shine,
The Libyc *Hammon* shrinks his horn,
In vain the *Tyrian* Maids their wounded *Thamuz* mourn.

XXIII

And sullen *Moloch* fled,
Hath left in shadows dred,
   His burning Idol all of blackest hue,
In vain with Cymbals ring,
They call the grisly king,
   In dismall dance about the furnace blue;
The brutish gods of *Nile* as fast,
Isis and *Orus*, and the Dog *Anubis* hast.

XXIV

Nor is *Osiris* seen
In *Memphian* Grove, or Green,
   Trampling the unshowr'd Grasse with lowings loud;
Nor can he be at rest
Within his sacred chest,
   Naught but profoundest Hell can be his shroud,
In vain with Timbrel'd Anthems dark
The sable-stoled Sorcerers bear his worshipt Ark.

XXV

He feels from *Juda*'s Land
The dredded Infants hand,
   The rayes of *Bethlehem* blind his dusky eyn;
Nor all the gods beside,
Longer dare abide,
   Not *Typhon* huge ending in snaky twine:
Our Babe to shew his Godhead true,
Can in his swadling bands controul the damned crew.

XXVI

So when the Sun in bed,
Curtain'd with cloudy red,
   Pillows his chin upon an Orient wave,
The flocking shadows pale,
Troop to th'infernall jail,
   Each fetter'd Ghost slips to his severall grave,
And the yellow-skirted *Fayes*,
Fly after the Night-steeds, leaving their Moon-lov'd maze.

XXVII

But see the Virgin blest,
Hath laid her Babe to rest,
   Time is our tedious Song should here have ending:
Heav'ns youngest teemed Star,
Hath fixt her polisht Car,
   Her sleeping Lord with Handmaid Lamp attending:
And all about the Courtly Stable,
Bright-harnest Angels sit in order serviceable.

John Milton
(1608–1674)

WENDY COPE
Additional Poems, IV, A. E. Housman

Dear Nicola, Paula and Alice,
Thank you for your letter. I am asked for my favourite poem at least once a
year and it would be boring to choose the same one every time. This, along
with several other poems by Housman, is certainly in my top twenty.

   We would all like to believe that love is stronger than death. Housman
can't go that far. Conceding that love doesn't last for ever, he has written a
very powerful love poem.

Yours sincerely,
WENDY COPE

Additional Poems

IV

It is no gift I tender,
   A loan is all I can;
But do not scorn the lender;
   Man gets no more from man.

Oh, mortal man may borrow
   What mortal man can lend;
And 'twill not end tomorrow,
   Though sure enough 'twill end.

If death and time are stronger,
   A love may yet be strong;
The world will last for longer
   But this will last for long.

A. E. Housman
(1859–1936)

MARTIN AMIS
From *Songs of Experience*, William Blake

Dear Nicola Hughes,
Thank you for your letter. In reply:

   As my twenty-first birthday neared, my then-stepmother Elizabeth Jane Howard cunningly asked me: 'What's your favourite stanza in English poetry?' Stanza three of the following poem subsequently appeared on the book-plate that was her present to me, above the words *ex libris*:

Songs of Experience
Introduction

Hear the voice of the Bard!
Who Present, Past, & Future sees
Whose ears have heard,
The Holy Word
That walk'd among the ancient trees,

Calling the lapsed Soul
And weeping in the evening dew
That might control,
The starry pole;
And fallen fallen light renew!

O Earth O Earth, return!
Arise from out the dewy grass;
Night is worn,
And the morn
Rises from the slumberous mass.

Turn away no more:
Why wilt thou turn away
The starry floor,
The watry shore
Is giv'n thee till the break of day.

William Blake
(1757–1827)

These lines – from Blake's 'Introduction' to the *Songs of Experience* – expressed my belief that poetry could awaken our prelapsarian soul. That belief is now inevitably weakened, though these lines will always make me remember what that belief felt like.

With best wishes,
MARTIN AMIS

ALAN HOLLINGHURST
Night Taxi, Thom Gunn

Dear Mss Hughes, Griffin and McEleney,
Thank you for your invitation to nominate a favourite poem for your *Lifelines* anthology. When I settled down to think what it might be, I realized that I had at least thirty favourite poems; but some of them were very long and some so obvious that they have doubtless been chosen by many other contributors. So in the end I set aside my Pope and Wordsworth and Tennyson and my Yeats and Hopkins and Heaney and Elizabeth Bishop, and picked a rather less well-known item by Thom Gunn (it comes from his book *The Passages of Joy* published by Faber and Faber in 1982).

I know of no more beautiful evocation of a city at night than that in 'Night Taxi'. In this case the city is San Francisco, where Thom Gunn lives, and to read these fluent but watchful lines is to see again its plunging hills and the glittering panorama of its bay. 'Loose but in control' might sum up the poet's technique: the voice is natural, unforced, though capable of a kind of exaltation; and the subject matter, if rare – even unprecedented – in poetry, is deliberately routine. Yet it seems to me a great elegiac poem, the stronger and the more poignant for the way it only glances at its theme, which I take to be the transience of experience, of sexual happiness, of our brief tenancy of our spot on earth. The poet, the taxi-driver, the dedicatee ('wherever he is'), have made their passage through this ghostly cityscape. The last lines hauntingly combine imagery of radiance and of dissolution.

With all good wishes for your project.

Yours sincerely,
ALAN HOLLINGHURST

Night Taxi

(For Rod Taylor, wherever he is)

Open city
uncluttered as a map.
I drive through empty streets
scoured by the winds
of midnight. My shift
is only beginning and I am fresh
and excitable, master of the taxi.
I relish my alert reflexes
where all else
is in hiding. I have
by default it seems
conquered me a city.

My first address: I
press the doorbell, I lean back
against the hood, my headlights
scalding a garage door, my engine
drumming in the driveway,
the only sound on the block.
There the fare finds me
like a date, jaunty,
shoes shined, I am
proud of myself, on my toes,
obliging but not subservient.

I take short cuts, picking up
speed, from time to time
I switch on the dispatcher's
litany of addresses,
China Basin to Twin Peaks,
Harrison Street to the Ocean.

I am thinking tonight
my fares are like affairs
– no, more like tricks to turn:
quick, lively, ending up
with a cash payment.
I do not anticipate a holdup.
I can make friendly small talk.
I do not go on about Niggers,
women drivers or the Chinese.
It's all on my terms but
I let them think it's on theirs.

Do I pass through the city
or does it pass through me?
I know I have to be loose,
like my light embrace of the wheel,
loose but in control
– though hour by hour I tighten
minutely in the routine,
smoking my palate to ash,
till the last hour of all
will be drudgery, nothing else.

I zip down Masonic Avenue,
the taxi sings beneath the streetlights
a song to the bare city, it is
my instrument, I woo with it,
bridegroom and conqueror.

I jump out to open the door,
fixing the cap on my head
to, you know, firm up my role,
and on my knuckle
feel a sprinkle of wet.

Glancing upward I see
high above the lamppost
but touched by its farthest light
a curtain of rain already blowing
against black eucalyptus tops.

Thom Gunn
(b. 1929)

BEN ELTON
Quote from *The Young Ones*, Cliff Richard

Dear Nicola, Paula and Alice,

To tell you the truth I have read very little poetry since leaving school. It is an omission I regret but one cannot do everything. I find it difficult enough keeping up with the prose I wish to read. Therefore I'm afraid I do not have a favourite poem. I know this is not a very helpful reply, but there you go. Were you to ask me to name my favourite poet I would answer Shakespeare, but to choose one piece from his endlessly inspiring work would be impossible.

Favourites aside, you might be surprised to hear that the single piece of verse that has most moved me is a quote from the lyric of Cliff Richard's old hit 'The Young Ones'. It was in 1984 when the *Young Ones* TV show which I had co-written was a big hit. Rik Mayall and I were on tour together. After the show we always signed autographs for those that wanted them. One night a mother came back with her son, he was about eleven and was, she explained, a colossal *Young Ones* fan, adding that he did not have long to live. The boy was embarrassed and tongue-tied, and of course nobody really knew what to say, so his mother asked Rik to write something for the boy on a tour poster. I did not envy Rik at that moment; what can you write, off the cuff, to a dying boy who adores you? In what I feel was a moment of inspiration Rik wrote a quote from Cliff's

old song which Rik had sung over the titles of the series. He wrote 'Young
Ones shouldn't be afraid'. The boy and his mother seemed much moved by
this thought, as indeed was I.

Not great poetry I'll admit, but good writing can sometimes be as much
about context as content and I shall always remember that line. As Noël
Coward (whose lyrics I also adore) once said, 'Strange how potent cheap
music *is*.'

Huge best wishes for the book.

Yours sincerely,
BEN ELTON

SEAMUS DEANE
A Disused Shed in Co. Wexford,
Derek Mahon

Dear Nicola, Paula, Alice,
Thank you for your letter and my apologies for the delay in replying. I don't
know that I have *a* favourite poem; but certainly among my favourites, I
would include Derek Mahon's 'A Disused Shed in Co. Wexford'.

The reasons? It is a poem that heartbreakingly dwells on and gives voice
to all those peoples and civilizations that have been lost and/or destroyed.
Since it is set in Ireland, with all the characteristic features of an Irish 'Big
House' ruin, it speaks with a special sharpness to the present moment and
the fear, rampant in Northern Ireland, of communities that fear they too
might perish and be lost, with none to speak for them.

Yours sincerely,
SEAMUS DEANE

A Disused Shed in Co. Wexford

Let them not forget us, the weak souls among the asphodels.
— Seferis, *Mythistorema*

(For J. G. Farrell)

Even now there are places where a thought might grow —
Peruvian mines, worked out and abandoned
To a slow clock of condensation,
An echo trapped for ever, and a flutter
Of wildflowers in the lift-shaft,
Indian compounds where the wind dances
And a door bangs with diminished confidence,
Lime crevices behind rippling rainbarrels,
Dog corners for bone burials;
And in a disused shed in Co. Wexford,

Deep in the grounds of a burnt-out hotel,
Among the bathtubs and the washbasins
A thousand mushrooms crowd to a keyhole.
This is the one star in their firmament
Or frames a star within a star.
What should they do there but desire?
So many days beyond the rhododendrons
With the world waltzing in its bowl of cloud,
They have learnt patience and silence
Listening to the rooks querulous in the high wood.

They have been waiting for us in a foetor
Of vegetable sweat since civil war days,
Since the gravel-crunching, interminable departure
Of the expropriated mycologist.
He never came back, and light since then
Is a keyhole rusting gently after rain.
Spiders have spun, flies dusted to mildew
And once a day, perhaps, they have heard something —
A trickle of masonry, a shout from the blue
Or a lorry changing gear at the end of the lane.

There have been deaths, the pale flesh flaking
Into the earth that nourished it;
And nightmares, born of these and the grim
Dominion of stale air and rank moisture.
Those nearest the door grow strong –
'Elbow room! Elbow room!'
The rest, dim in a twilight of crumbling
Utensils and broken flower-pots, groaning
For their deliverance, have been so long
Expectant that there is left only the posture.

A half century, without visitors, in the dark –
Poor preparation for the cracking lock
And creak of hinges. Magi, moonmen,
Powdery prisoners of the old regime,
Web-throated, stalked like triffids, racked by drought
And insomnia, only the ghost of a scream
At the flash-bulb firing squad we wake them with
Shows there is life yet in their feverish forms.
Grown beyond nature now, soft food for worms,
They lift frail heads in gravity and good faith.

They are begging us, you see, in their wordless way,
To do something, to speak on their behalf
Or at least not to close the door again.
Lost people of Treblinka and Pompeii!
'Save us, save us,' they seem to say,
'Let the god not abandon us
Who have come so far in darkness and in pain.
We too had our lives to live.
You with your light meter and relaxed itinerary,
Let not our naive labours have been in vain!'

Derek Mahon
(b. 1941)

JAMES SIMMONS
A Toccata of Galuppi's,
Robert Browning

Dear Friends,

No one can have an absolute favourite poem but tonight mine would be 'A Toccata of Galuppi's' by Robert Browning. Shakespeare is my favourite author but I presume you do not want an extract from his plays. Poetry – language – with Shakespeare is used to illuminate human predicaments and the oddities of the whole human enterprise. So it is in Browning's poems, though he brings it off less often. In my own work I have tried to follow their example and held a line against a depressing sea of modern poetry that is either too oblique and 'clever' or too personal and tedious. In this poem Browning takes a period in history and feels his way into it until it reads like personal experience, and thus it becomes his own history and our history, and anyone who reads it attentively will be saddened and inspired.

Good luck with your work,
JAMES SIMMONS

A Toccata of Galuppi's

I

Oh, Galuppi, Baldassaro, this is very sad to find!
I can hardly misconceive you; it would prove me deaf and
   blind;
But although I take your meaning, 'tis with such a heavy
   mind!

II

Here you come with your old music, and here's all the
   good it brings.
What, they lived once thus at Venice where the merchants
   were the kings,
Where Saint Mark's is, where the Doges used to wed the
   sea with rings?

Aye, because the sea's the street there; and 'tis arched by
   . . . what you call
. . . Shylock's bridge with houses on it, where they kept
   the carnival:
I was never out of England — it's as if I saw it all.

IV

Did young people take their pleasure when the sea was
   warm in May?
Balls and masks begun at midnight, burning ever to
   midday,
When they made up fresh adventures for the morrow, do
   you say?

V

Was a lady such a lady, cheeks so round and lips so red —
On her neck the small face buoyant, like a bellflower on
   its bed
O'er the breast's superb abundance where a man might
   base his head?

VI

Well, and it was graceful of them — they'd break talk off
   and afford
— She, to bite her mask's black velvet — he, to finger on his
   sword,
While you sat and played toccatas, stately at the
   clavichord?

VII

What? Those lesser thirds so plaintive, sixths diminished,
   sigh on sigh,
Told them something? Those suspensions, those solutions
   — 'Must we die?'
Those commiserating sevenths — 'Life might last! we can
   but try!'

VIII

'Were you happy?' – 'Yes.' – 'And are you still as happy?'
   – 'Yes. And you?'
– 'Then, more kisses!' – 'Did *I* stop them, when a million
   seemed so few?'
Hark, the dominant's persistence till it must be answered
   to!

IX

So, an octave struck the answer. Oh, they praised you, I
   dare say!
'Brave Galuppi! that was music; good alike at grave and
   gay!
I can always leave off talking when I hear a master play!'

X

Then they left you for their pleasure: till in due time, one
   by one,
Some with lives that came to nothing, some with deeds as
   well undone,
Death stepped tacitly and took them where they never see
   the sun.

XI

But when I sit down to reason, think to take my stand nor
   swerve,
While I triumph o'er a secret wrung from nature's close
   reserve,
In you come with your cold music till I creep through
   every nerve.

XII

Yes, you, like a ghostly cricket, creaking where a house
   was burned:
'Dust and ashes, dead and done with, Venice spent what
   Venice earned.
The soul, doubtless, is immortal – where a soul can be
   discerned.

XIII

'Yours for instance: you know physics, something of
   geology,
Mathematics are your pastime; souls shall rise in their
   degree;
Butterflies may dread extinction – you'll not die, it cannot
   be!

XIV

'As for Venice and her people, merely born to bloom and
   drop,
Here on earth they bore their fruitage, mirth and folly
   were the crop:
What of soul was left, I wonder, when the kissing had to
   stop?

XV

'Dust and ashes!' So you creak it, and I want the heart to
   scold.
Dear dead women, with such hair, too – what's become of
   all the gold
Used to hang and brush their bosoms? I feel chilly and
   grown old.

Robert Browning
(1812–1889)

NEIL RUDENSTINE
To Autumn, John Keats

Dear Ms Hughes et al.:
I am happy to contribute to *Lifelines*, but I should say that I have no single
favorite poem – and many of the poems that are most important to me are
not quite 'poems' in the usual sense, and are much too long for an

anthology. *The Iliad, The Canterbury Tales, The Divine Comedy, Paradise Lost*, and many other works would fall into this category.

Poems shift their meanings – and their importance – at different times, in different periods of our life, and on different occasions. So no single poem – or even a few – will really be adequate. Choosing one poem is impossible, but it would be possible at least to say that John Keats's ode 'To Autumn' is one of the very great poems in English, and is very important to me personally: it says much about growth and maturity; age and death and bleakness; richness and fruition and indulgence; and finally about the way in which all these perceptions, feelings and ideas can be held together in consciousness, in such a way as to evoke their power and yet reconcile and give resolution to what may seem irreconcilable in them. It also does this, not so much by explicit statement, but by the wonderfully modulated tones of the poet, the images captured, and the implicit meanings that those images suggest.

Sincerely,
NEIL RUDENSTINE

To Autumn

I

Season of mists and mellow fruitfulness,
    Close bosom friend of the maturing sun,
Conspiring with him how to load and bless
    With fruit the vines that round the thatch-eves run:
To bend with apples the mossed cottage-trees,
    And fill all fruit with ripeness to the core;
        To swell the gourd, and plump the hazel shells
    With a sweet kernel; to set budding more,
And still more, later flowers for the bees,
Until they think warm days will never cease,
    For summer has o'er-brimmed their clammy cells.

II

Who hath not seen thee oft amid thy store?
    Sometimes whoever seeks abroad may find
Thee sitting careless on a granary floor,
    Thy hair soft-lifted by the winnowing wind;

Or on a half-reaped furrow sound asleep,
　　Drowsed with the fume of poppies, while thy hook
　　　Spares the next swath and all its twinèd flowers;
And sometimes like a gleaner thou dost keep
　　Steady thy laden head across a brook;
　　Or by a cyder-press, with patient look,
　　　Thou watchest the last oozings hours by hours.

III
Where are the songs of spring? Aye, where are they?
　　Think not of them, thou hast thy music too –
While barrèd clouds bloom the soft-dying day,
　　And touch the stubble-plains with rosy hue.
Then in a wailful choir the small gnats mourn
　　Among the river sallows, borne aloft
　　　Or sinking as the light wind lives or dies;
And full-grown lambs loud bleat from hilly bourn;
　　Hedge-crickets sing; and now with treble soft
　　The red-breast whistles from a garden-croft;
　　　And gathering swallows twitter in the skies.

　　　　　　　　　　　　　　　　　John Keats
　　　　　　　　　　　　　　　　　(1795–1821)

DAVID LEAVITT
The Moose, Elizabeth Bishop

Dear Nicola, Paula and Alice,
Thanks very much for your letter. The poem I've decided to send you is
'The Moose' by Elizabeth Bishop. It's rather a long poem as you can see.
　I think the reason I love this poem so much is because magically, it
articulates everything that seems to me to be important about experiences –
how the 'homely' can so easily glide into the 'otherworldly'; how a moose,

caught in the twin beams of a Boston-bound bus, can transcend its own earthliness to become something both more and less than human, generating a 'sweet sensation of joy'. There is a calmness to the language of this poem, an ease and simplicity that belies the reality of its making. (It took Bishop years to compose.) And it contains some of the most breathtaking descriptions of nature that I've ever read. (In particular, I shall never forget 'the sweet peas cling to their wet white string'.)

With very best wishes,
DAVID LEAVITT

('The Moose' was also Derek Mahon's choice. The poem appears in full on p. 44.)

DECLAN KIBERD
The Dead Wife, ascribed to
Muireadhach Albanach

Dear Wesley Students,
Thanks for your letter. My favourite poem is an Irish Bardic lyric 'M'Anam do Sgar Riomsa A-raoir', to be found in Osborn Bergin's *Irish Bardic Poetry* (ed. F. Kelly) with English version.

It is the most moving elegy I have ever read, evoking the poet's dead wife with a unique blend of tenderness and formality. The lines throb with painful desire, and yet the whole utterance has been dramatically disciplined, so that the reader feels overcome by the energetic reticence of a speaker who is – for all his expressive power – leaving the deepest things unsaid. Most of the Bardic poems of Gaelic Ireland were drearily formulaic in theme and in technique, and so I was rather bored when studying them in college; but I can still recall the explosion of feeling when first I heard this poem, read by Professor David Greene not long after the death of his own wife. Every time I reread it, I feel that it is the work of a poet who knows that love is the only possible challenge to time. His wife, who was a joy to him in life, has become all the more mysterious in death. In saying that his soul separated from his body last night, he seems to suggest that the male and female will only become a single person again when they are reunited in heaven.

All good wishes for your project,
DECLAN KIBERD

'M' Anam do Sgar Riomsa A-raoir'

M'anam do sgar riomsa a-raoir,
    calann ghlan dob ionnsa i n-uaigh;
rugadh bruinne maordha mín
    is aonbhla lín uime uainn.

Do tógbhadh sgath aobhdha fhionn
    a-mach ar an bhfaongha bhfann:
laogh mo chridhise do chrom,
    craobh throm an tighise thall.

M'aonar a-nocht damhsa, a Dhé,
    olc an saoghal camsa ad-chí;
dob álainn trom an taoibh naoi
    do bhaoi sonn a-raoir, a Rí.

Truagh leam an leabasa thiar,
    mo pheall seadasa dhá snámh;
tárramair corp seada saor
    is folt claon, a leaba, id lár.

Do bhí duine go ndreich moill
    ina luighe ar leigh mo phill;
gan bharamhail acht bláth cuill
    don sgáth duinn bhanamhail bhinn.

Maol Mheadha na malach ndonn
    mo dhabhach mheadha a-raon rom;
mo chridhe an sgáth do sgar riom
    bláth mhionn arna car do chrom.

Táinig an chlí as ar gcuing,
   agus dí ráinig mar roinn:
corp idir dá aisil inn
   ar dtocht don fhinn mhaisigh mhoill.

Leath mo throigheadh, leath mo thaobh,
   a dreach mar an droighean bán,
níor dhísle neach dhí ná dhún,
   leath mo shúl í, leath mo lámh.

Leath mo chuirp an choinneal naoi;
   's gúirt riom do roinneadh, a Rí;
agá labhra is meirtneach mé –
   dob é ceirtleath m'anma í.

Mo chéadghrádh a dearc mhall mhór,
   déadbhán agus cam a cliabh:
nochar bhean a colann caomh
   ná a taobh ré fear romham riamh.

Fiche bliadhna inne ar-aon,
   fá binne gach bliadhna ar nglór,
go rug éinleanabh déag dhún,
   an ghéag úr mhéirleabhar mhór.

Gé tú, nocha n-oilim ann,
   ó do thoirinn ar gcnú chorr;
ar sgaradh dár roghrádh rom,
   falamh lom an domhnán donn.

Ón ló do sáidheadh cleath corr
   im theach nochar raidheadh rum –
ní thug aoighe d'ortha ann
   dá barr naoidhe dhorcha dhunn.

A dhaoine, ná coisgidh damh;
   faoidhe ré cloistin ní col;
táinig luinnchreach lom 'nar dteagh –
   an bhruithneach gheal donn ar ndol.

Is é rug uan í 'na ghrúg,
   Rí na sluagh is Rí na ród;
beag an cion do chúl na ngéag
   a héag ó a fior go húr óg.

Ionmhain lámh bhog do bhí sonn,
   a Rí na gclog is na gceall:
ach! an lámh nachar logh mionn,
   crádh liom gan a cor fám cheann.

(Ascribed to Muireadhach Albanach)
(*fl.* early 13th cent.)

The Dead Wife

My soul parted from me last night; a pure body that was dear is in the grave; a gentle stately bosom has been taken from me with one linen shroud about it.

A white comely blossom has been plucked from the feeble bending stalk; my own heart's darling has drooped, the fruitful branch of yonder house.

I am alone tonight, O God; evil is this crooked world that Thou seest; lovely was the weight of the young body that was here last night, O King.

Sad for me (to behold) yonder couch, my long pallet . . . ; we have seen a tall noble form with waving tresses upon thee, O couch.

A woman of gentle countenance lay upon one side of my pallet; there was naught save the hazel-blossom like to the dark shadow, womanly and sweet-voiced.

Maol Mheadha of the dark brows, my mead-vessel beside me; my heart the shadow that has parted from me, the flower of jewels after being planted has drooped.

My body has passed from my control, and has fallen to her share;
I am a body in two pieces since the lovely bright and gentle one is gone.

She was one of my two feet, one of my sides – her countenance like the white-thorn; none belonged to her more than to me, she was one of my eyes, one of my hands.

She was the half of my body, the fresh torch; harshly have I been treated, O King; I am faint as I tell it – she was the very heart of my soul.

Her large gentle eye was my first love, her bosom was curved and white as ivory; her fair body belonged to no man before me.

Twenty years we spent together; sweeter was our converse each year; she bore to me eleven children, the tall fresh lithe-fingered branch.

Though I am alive, I am no more, since my smooth hazel-nut is fallen; since my dear love parted from me, the dark world is empty and bare.

From the day that a smooth post was fixed in my house it has not been told me – no guest laid a spell therein upon her youthful dark brown hair.

O men, check me not; the sound of weeping is not forbidden; bare and cruel ruin has come into my house – the bright brown glowing one is gone.

It is the King of Hosts and the King of Roads who has taken her away in His displeasure; little was the fault of the branching tresses that she should die and leave her husband while fresh and young.

Dear the soft hand that was here, O King of bells and churchyards; alas! the hand that never swore (false) oath, 'tis torment to me that it is not placed under my head.

(Translated by Osborn Bergin)

SUE LAWLEY
The Forsaken Merman,
Matthew Arnold

Dear Nicola, Paula and Alice,
Thank you for asking me to make a contribution to *Lifelines IV*. My choice
of poem would be Matthew Arnold's 'The Forsaken Merman'.

I don't think this is the most important poem that Arnold ever wrote but
it is one which I discovered aged about eleven and it has stayed with me
ever since. I recently introduced my daughter, also now eleven years old, to
it and she seems equally moved by this rather pathetic tale of a merman
who married a mortal but was ultimately forsaken.

I think it is a perfect narrative poem which carries you along rhyth-
mically, holds your interest, enables you to identify with the equivocations
of the hero and, finally, leaves you with a feeling of great sadness for his loss.
Not a word is wasted (I could probably quote most of them to you) and
not an eye is dry.

Good luck with the book.

> Best wishes,
> Yours sincerely,
> SUE LAWLEY

The Forsaken Merman

Come, dear children, let us away;
Down and away below!
Now my brothers call from the bay,
Now the great winds shoreward blow,
Now the salt tides seaward flow;
Now the wild white horses play,
Champ and chafe and toss in the spray.
Children dear, let us away!
This way, this way!

Call her once before you go –
Call once yet!
In a voice that she will know:
'Margaret! Margaret!'
Children's voices should be dear
(Call once more) to a mother's ear;
Children's voices, wild with pain –
Surely she will come again!
Call her once and come away;
This way, this way!
'Mother dear, we cannot stay!
The wild white horses foam and fret.'
Margaret! Margaret!

Come, dear children, come away down;
Call no more!
One last look at the white-walled town,
And the little grey church on the windy shore,
Then come down!
She will not come though you call all day;
Come away, come away!

Children dear, was it yesterday-
We heard the sweet bells over the bay?
In the caverns where we lay,
Through the surf and through the swell,
The far-off sound of a silver bell?
Sand-strewn caverns, cool and deep,
Where the winds are all asleep;
Where the spent lights quiver and gleam,
Where the salt weed sways in the stream,
Where the sea beasts, ranged all round,
Feed in the ooze of their pasture ground;
Where the sea snakes coil and twine,
Dry their mail and bask in the brine;
Where great whales come sailing by,
Sail and sail, with unshut eye,
Round the world for ever and aye?
When did music come this way?
Children dear, was it yesterday?

Children dear, was it yesterday
(Call yet once) that she went away?
Once she sate with you and me,
On a red gold throne in the heart of the sea,
And the youngest sate on her knee.
She combed its bright hair, and she tended it well,
When down swung the sound of a far-off bell.
She sighed, she looked up through the clear green sea;
She said: 'I must go, for my kinsfolk pray
In the little grey church on the shore today.
'Twill be Easter time in the world – ah me!
And I lose my poor soul, Merman! here with thee.'
I said: 'Go up, dear heart, through the waves;
Say thy prayer, and come back to the kind sea caves!'
She smiled, she went up through the surf in the bay.
Children dear, was it yesterday?

Children dear, were we long alone?
'The sea grows stormy, the little ones moan;
Long prayers,' I said, 'in the world they say;
Come!' I said; and we rose through the surf in the bay.
We went up the beach, by the sandy down
Where the sea stocks bloom, to the white-walled town;
Through the narrow paved streets, where all was still,
To the little grey church on the windy hill.
From the church came a murmur of folk at their prayers,
But we stood without in the cold blowing airs.
We climbed on the graves, on the stones worn with rains,
And we gazed up the aisle through the small leaded panes.
She sate by the pillar; we saw her clear:
'Margaret, hist! come quick, we are here!
Dear heart,' I said, 'we are long alone;
The sea grows stormy, the little ones moan.'
But, ah, she gave me never a look,
For her eyes were sealed to the holy book!
Loud prays the priest; shut stands the door.
Come away, children, call no more!
Come away, come down, call no more!

Down, down, down!
Down to the depths of the sea!
She sits at her wheel in the humming town,
Singing most joyfully.
Hark what she sings: 'O joy, o joy,
For the humming street, and the child with its toy!
For the priest, and the bell, and the holy well;
For the wheel where I spun,
And the blessed light of the sun!'
And so she sings her fill,
Singing most joyfully,
Till the spindle drops from her hand,
And the whizzing wheel stands still.
She steals to the window, and looks at the sand,
And over the sand at the sea;
And her eyes are set in a stare;
And anon there breaks a sigh,
And anon there drops a tear,
From a sorrow-clouded eye,
And a heart sorrow-laden,
A long, long sigh;
For the cold strange eyes of a little Mermaiden
And the gleam of her golden hair.

   Come away, away children;
Come children, come down!
The hoarse wind blows coldly;
Lights shine in the town.
She will start from her slumber
When gusts shake the door;
She will hear the winds howling,
Will hear the waves roar.
We shall see, while above us
The waves roar and whirl,
A ceiling of amber,
A pavement of pearl.
Singing: 'Here came a mortal,
But faithless was she!
And alone dwell for ever
The kings of the sea.

But, children, at midnight,
When soft the winds blow,
When clear falls the moonlight,
When spring tides are low;
When sweet airs come seaward
From heaths starred with broom,
And high rocks throw mildly
On the blanched sands a gloom;
Up the still, glistening beaches,
Up the creek we will hie,
Over the banks of bright seaweed
The ebb tide leaves dry.
We will gaze, from the sand hills,
At the white, sleeping town;
At the church on the hillside –
And then come back down.
Singing: 'There dwells a loved one,
But cruel is she!
She left lonely for ever
The kings of the sea.'

Matthew Arnold
(1822–1888)

HUGO HAMILTON
The Mirror, Michael Davitt

Dear Editors,
Many thanks for inviting me to submit my favourite poem.

I have selected a poem by Michael Davitt which has been translated from the Irish by his fellow poet Paul Muldoon with the title 'The Mirror'. The poem and its translation both appear in *Selected Poems 1968–1984*.

'The Mirror' is the clearest description I've ever heard of the father and son relationship, the son taking up the job so unwisely taken on by the father. The grief for his father's death is declared by default, almost in a note of anger at his father taking down the mirror without the son's help. There is an image of the father as a stranger, a man recently retired from CIE, breathing life into his son through the mirror as they put it back up again together. It's how I felt about my own father.

Yours sincerely,
HUGO HAMILTON

An Scáthán

(I gcuimhne m'athar)

I

Níorbh é m'athair níos mó é
ach ba mise a mhacsan;
paradacsa fuar a d'fháisceas,
dealbh i gculaith Dhomhnaigh
a cuireadh an lá dár gcionn.

Dhein sé an-lá deora, seirí
fuiscí, ceapairí feola is tae.
Bhí seanchara leis ag eachtraí
faoi sciurd lae a thugadar
ar Eochaill sna tríochaidí
is gurbh é a chéad pháirtí é
i seirbhís Chorcaí/An Sciobairín
amach sna daicheadaí.
Bhí dornán cártaí Aifrinn
ar mhatal an tseomra suí
ina gcorrán thart ar vás gloine,
a bhronntanas scoir ó CIE.

II

Níorbh eol dom go ceann dhá lá
gurbh é an scáthán a mharaigh é . . .

An seanscáthán ollmhór Victeoiriach
leis an bhfráma ornáideach bréagórga
a bhí romhainn sa tigh trí stór

nuair a bhogamar isteach ón tuath.
Bhínn scanraithe roimhe: go sciorrfadh
anuas den bhfalla is go slogfadh mé
d'aon tromanáil i lár na hoíche . . .

Ag maisiú an tseomra chodlata dó
d'ardaigh sé an scáthán anuas
dan lámh chúnta a iarraidh;
ar ball d'iompaigh dath na cré air,
an oíche sin phléasc a chroí.

III

Mar a chuirfí de gheasa orm
thugas faoin jab a chríochnú:
an folús macallach a pháipéarú,
an fhuinneog ard a phéinteáil,
an doras marbhlainne
a scríobadh. Nuair a rugas ar an scáthán
sceimhlíos. Bhraitheas é ag análú tríd.
Chuala é ag rá i gcogar téiglí:
I'll give you a hand, here.

Is d'ardaíomar an scáthán thar n-ais in airde
os cionn an tinteáin,
m'athair á choinneáil
fad a dheineas-sa é a dhaingniú
le dhá thairne.

Michael Davitt
(b. 1950)

The Mirror

(In memory of my father)

I

He was no longer my father
but I was still his son;
I would get to grips with that cold paradox,

the remote figure in his Sunday best
who was buried the next day.

A great day for tears, snifters of sherry,
whiskey, beef sandwiches, tea.
An old mate of his was recounting
their day excursion
to Youghal in the Thirties,
how he was his first partner
on the Cork/Skibbereen route
in the late Forties.
There was a splay of Mass cards
on the sitting-room mantelpiece
which formed a crescent round a glass vase,
his retirement present from CIE.

II

I didn't realize till two days later
it was the mirror took his breath away . . .

The monstrous old Victorian mirror
with the ornate gilt frame
we had found in the three-storey house
when we moved in from the country.
I was afraid that it would sneak
down from the wall and swallow me up
in one gulp in the middle of the night . . .

While he was decorating the bedroom
he had taken down the mirror
without asking for help;
soon he turned the colour of terracotta
and his heart broke that night.

III

There was nothing for it
but to set about finishing the job,
papering over the cracks,
painting the high window,

stripping the door, like the door of a crypt.
When I took hold of the mirror
I had a fright. I imagined him breathing through it.
I heard him say in a reassuring whisper:
I'll give you a hand, here.

And we lifted the mirror back in position
above the fireplace,
my father holding it steady
while I drove home
the two nails.

(Translated by Paul Muldoon)

MICHAEL BLUMENTHAL
The Painter Dreaming in the Scholar's House, Howard Nemerov

Dear Nicola, Paula and Alice,

I'm, of course, happy to participate in your *Lifelines* project, and flattered to have been asked. I'm a tad unhappier, I must admit, at being asked to identify my 'favourite' poem, as I have no such thing, really, only poems I love, as people, the intensity and depth of whose call to me on particular days and in particular moods varies, yet all of which I love dearly, and for different – albeit often intersecting – reasons. ALL of them are equally my favourites.

In any event, I appreciate and support what you're doing, and so herewith enclose *today's* choice for my 'favourite' poem – 'The Painter Dreaming in the Scholar's House', by our own late Poet Laureate and my good friend, Howard Nemerov.

I love this poem dearly for how beautifully it seeks to create a world (the world of the poem) in which, to paraphrase the poet, spirit and sense are not at odds. Its iambic pentameter is almost effortless-seeming, and as light-handed and deft (I think) as Wordsworth's or Frost's. In this poem, clarity and mystery cohabit beautifully, neither at the expense of the other. And, very delicately, never pompously or self-consciously, it dares to take on the 'great' themes – the conflict of spirit and sense, the transience of life itself and of its small but meaningful exercises of virtue, the hoped-for redemptions of art as an act of faith, the need for an eye that is 'clarified towards charity'. When I first heard it read, some fifteen years ago at the Library of Congress, it made me weep. And it *still* makes me weep . . . But 'it never breaks up its lines to weep', as a poem never should. And though, quite clearly, it is a poem that *thinks*, it is also a poem that thinks as Roethke said a poet should: *by feeling*.

I hope, and trust, that this will be helpful to you, and wish you all the best for continued success on your very worthwhile project.

Sincerely,
MICHAEL BLUMENTHAL

The Painter Dreaming in the Scholar's House

(In memory of the painters Paul Klee and Paul Terence Feeley)

I

The painter's eye follows relation out.
His work is not to paint the visible,
He says, it is to render visible.

Being a man, and not a god, he stands
Already in a world of sense, from which
He borrows, to begin with, mental things
Chiefly, the abstract elements of language:
The point, the line, the plane, the colors and
The geometric shapes. Of these he spins
Relation out, he weaves its fabric up
So that it speaks darkly, as music does
Singing the secret history of the mind.
And when in this the visible world appears,
As it does do, mountain, flower, cloud, and tree,
All haunted here and there with the human face,
It happens as by accident, although
The accident is of design. It is because

Language first rises from the speechless world
That the painterly intelligence
Can say correctly that he makes his world,
Not imitates the one before his eyes.
Hence the delightsome gardens, the dark shores,
The terrifying forests where nightfall
Enfolds a lost and tired traveler.

And hence the careless crowd deludes itself
By likening his hieroglyphic signs
And secret alphabets to the drawing of a child.
That likeness is significant the other side
Of what they see, for his simplicities
Are not the first ones, but the furthest ones,
Final refinements of his thought made visible.
He is the painter of the human mind
Finding and faithfully reflecting the mindfulness
That is in things, and not the things themselves.

For such a man, art is an act of faith:
Prayer the study of it, as Blake says,
And praise the practice; nor does he divide
Making from teaching, or from theory.
The three are one, and in his hours of art
There shines a happiness through darkest themes,
As though spirit and sense were not at odds.

II

The painter as an allegory of the mind
At genesis. He takes a burlap bag,
Tears it open and tacks it on a stretcher.
He paints it black because, as he has said,
Everything looks different on black.

Suppose the burlap bag to be the universe,
And black because its volume is the void
Before the stars were. At the painter's hand
Volume becomes one-sidedly a surface,
And all his depths are on the face of it.

Against this flat abyss, this groundless ground
Of zero thickness stretched against the cold
Dark silence of the Absolutely Not,
Material worlds arise, the colored earths
And oil of plants that imitate the light.

They imitate the light that is in thought,
For the mind relates to thinking as the eye
Relates to light. Only because the world
Already is a language can the painter speak
According to the grammar of the ground.

It is archaic speech, that has not yet
Divided out its cadences in words;
It is a language for the oldest spells
About how some thoughts rose into the mind
While others, stranger still, sleep in the world.

So grows the garden green, the sun vermilion.
He sees the rose flame up and fade and fall.
And be the same rose still, the radiant in red.
He paints his language, and his language is
The theory of what the painter thinks.

III

The painter's eye attends to death and birth
Together, seeing a single energy
Momently manifest in every form,
As in the tree the growing of the tree
Exploding from the seed not more nor less
Than from the void condensing down and in,
Summoning sun and rain. He views the tree,
The great tree standing in the garden, say,
As thrusting downward its vast spread and weight,
Growing its green height from dark watered earth,
And as suspended weightless in the sky,
Haled forth and held up by the hair of its head.
He follows through the flowing of the forms
From the divisions of the trunk out to
The veinings of the leaf, and the leaf's fall.

His pencil meditates the many in the one
After the method in the confluence of rivers,
The running of ravines on mountainsides,
And in the deltas of the nerves; he sees
How things must be continuous with themselves
As with whole worlds that they themselves are not,
In order that they may be so transformed.
He stands where the eternity of thought
Opens upon perspective time and space;
He watches mind become incarnate; then
   He paints the tree.

IV

These thoughts have chiefly been about the painter Klee,
About how he in our hard time might stand to us
Especially whose lives concern themselves with learning
As patron of the practical intelligence of art,
And thence as model, modest and humorous in sufferings,
For all research that follows spirit where it goes.

That there should be much goodness in the world,
Much kindness and intelligence, candor and charm,
And that it all goes down in the dust after a while,
This is a subject for the steadiest meditations
Of the heart and mind, as for the tears
That clarify the eye toward charity.

So may it be to all of us, that at some times
In this bad time when faith in study seems to fail,
And when impatience in the street and still despair at
   home
Divide the mind to rule it, there shall some comfort come
From the remembrance of so deep and clear a life as his
Whom I have thought of, for the wholeness of his mind,
As the painter dreaming in the scholar's house,
His dream an emblem to us of the life of thought,
The same dream that then flared before intelligence
When light first went forth looking for the eye.

Howard Nemerov
(1920–1991)

MIROSLAV HOLUB
Masterpiece, Miroslav Holub
Resurrection, Vladimir Holan

Dear Nicola Hughes,
Dear Paula Griffin,
Dear Alice McEleney,
I am not sure that I read your letter correctly: should it be *my* poem or any poem?

I have chosen one of my own poems for the only reason that I must give my own poems more thought and that I must spend much more time with them.

The poem 'Masterpiece' was published in the *London Poetry Review* last fall. It was written recently and therefore belongs to my actual self. It is childish enough to be a real poem and, which is most important, is not that gloomy as most poems written today anywhere.

Best wishes to your project,

Yours,
MIROSLAV HOLUB

Masterpiece

The only masterpiece
I ever created
was a picture of the moth Thysania agrippina
in pastel on grey paper.

Because I was never
much good at painting. The essence of art
is that we aren't very good at it.

The moth Thysania agrippina
rose from the stiff grey paper
with outstretched, comb-like antennae,

with a plush bottom resembling the buttocks
of the pigwidgeons of Hieronymus Bosch,
with thin legs on a shrunken chest
like those on Breughel's grotesque figures
in 'Dulle Griet', it turned into Dulle Griet
with a bundle of pots and pans in her bony hand,

it turned into Bodhiddharma
with long sleeves,

it was Ying or Shade
and Yang or Light, Chwei or Darkness
and Ming or Glow, it had
the black colour of water, the ochre colour of earth,
the blue colour of wood.

I was as proud of it as an Antwerp councillor,
or the Tenth Patriarch from the Yellow River,

I sprinkled it with shellac, which is
the oath that painters swear on Goethe's Science of
    Colours,

and then the art teacher took it to his study

and I forgot all about it
the way Granny used to forget
her dentures in a glass.

Miroslav Holub
(b. 1923)
(Translated by Dana Hábová and David Young)

[When Miroslav Holub read *Lifelines IV* he felt that he had misunderstood
the request and was uneasy about having submitted one of his own poems.
He asked if the following letter and choice might also be included in the
collected and selected editions.]

Dear Paula, Nicola and Alice,
The term 'favourite poem' is very plastic, almost like the sea-god Proteus.
The answer, for me, depends even on the nature of the person who asked.

For three beautiful girls, I would rather pick something very manly, like something from Ted Hughes or Galway Kinnell.

But, realizing I have to answer as a Czech among Irish and English people, Vladimir Holan occurs to me, and this poem which was so close to our Poetry of Everyday that it reads like something deeply related, something I would wish to have written.

MIROSLAV HOLUB

Resurrection

Is it true that after this life of ours we shall one day be
    awakened
by a terrifying clamour of trumpets?
Forgive me, God, but I console myself
that the beginning and resurrection of all of us dead
will simply be announced by the crowing of the cock.

After that we'll remain lying down a while . . .
The first to get up
will be Mother . . . We'll hear her
quietly laying the fire,
quietly putting the kettle on the stove
and cosily taking the teapot out of the cupboard.
We'll be home once more.

Vladimir Holan
(1905–1980)
(Translated by George Theiner)

NOTES ON THE CONTRIBUTORS
(in alphabetical order)

FLEUR ADCOCK (p. 36)
Poet (*Selected Poems*, *The Incident Book*, *Time-zones*), translator, critic and anthologist.

SIR KINGSLEY AMIS (p. 106)
Novelist (*Lucky Jim*, *The Old Devils*, *The Russian Girl*), poet (*Bright November*), anthologist and author of autobiographical and critical works.

MARTIN AMIS (p. 172)
Novelist (*Money*, *Time's Arrow*) and essayist (*The Moronic Inferno*, *Einstein's Monsters*).

LORD JEFFREY ARCHER (p. 55)
Novelist (*Kane and Abel*, *As the Crow Flies*) and politician.

SIMON ARMITAGE (p. 143)
Poet (*Zoom!*, *Kid*).

MARGARET ATWOOD (p. 89)
Canadian novelist (*The Handmaid's Tale*, *Cat's Eye*), short-story writer and poet (*True Stories*, *Interlunar*).

JOHN BANVILLE (p. 13)
Novelist (*Kepler*, *The Book of Evidence*) and literary editor of the *Irish Times*.

LYNN BARBER (p. 136)
Columnist for the *Independent on Sunday*, feature writer for *Vanity Fair* and author of *Mostly Men*.

JULIAN BARNES (p. 150)
Novelist (*Flaubert's Parrot*, *A History of the World in Ten and a Half Chapters*, *Talking It Over*).

JOHN BAYLEY (p. 127)
Scholar, critic, author (*Tolstoy and the Novel*, *The Romantic Survival: A Study in Poetic Evolution*) and Professor Emeritus at Oxford.

MAEVE BINCHY (p. 56)
Novelist (*Light a Penny Candle*, *Firefly Summer*, *The Copper Beech*), playwright, journalist, critic and columnist with the *Irish Times*.

MICHAEL BLUMENTHAL (p. 199)

American poet (*Days We Would Rather Know*, *Laps*) and Briggs-Copeland Assistant Professor at Harvard University.

EAVAN BOLAND (p. 2)

Poet (*Night Feed*, *Outside History*).

CLARE BOYLAN (p. 85)

Novelist (*Black Baby*, *Holy Pictures*, *Home Rule*) short-story writer (*A Nail on the Head*, *Concerning Virgins*) and journalist.

KENNETH BRANAGH (p. 154)

Actor and director. Played Henry V on stage with the Royal Shakespeare Company and on screen. A director of The Renaissance Theatre Company.

RICHARD BRANSON (p. 80)

Businessman. Chairperson and founder of The Virgin Group.

BARBARA BUSH (p. 114)

America's former First Lady.

A. S. BYATT, CBE (p. 93)

Novelist (*The Virgin in the Garden*, *Possession*), broadcaster and critic (*Unruly Times: Wordsworth and Coleridge*, *Poetry and Life*).

GAY BYRNE (p. 33)

Broadcaster. Presenter of *The Late, Late Show* on RTE television – the longest-running talk-show in the history of television. Author of *The Time of My Life: An Autobiography*.

AMY CLAMPITT (p. 107)

American poet (*The Kingfisher*, *Westward*).

ANTHONY CLARE (p. 133)

Psychiatrist, broadcaster, author and presenter of *In the Psychiatrist's Chair* on BBC Radio 4.

ADAM CLAYTON (p. 99)

Musician. Member of U2.

SHANE CONNAUGHTON (p. 139)

Novelist (*A Border Station*, *The Run of the Country*) and writer of screen-plays.

JILLY COOPER (p. 138)

Novelist (*Rivals*, *Polo*) and journalist.

WENDY COPE (p. 171)

Poet (*Making Cocoa for Kingsley Amis*, *Serious Concerns*).

ANTHONY CRONIN (p. 155)

Poet (*The End of the Modern World*) and scholar (*No Laughing Matter: The Life and Times of Flann O'Brien*). Chairman and founder of Aosdána.

CYRIL CUSACK (p. 25)

Actor, playwright, poet (*Between the Acts and Other Poems*) and author of autobiographical and critical works.

NIAMH CUSACK (p. 125)

Actor. Has played Desdemona with the Royal Shakespeare Company and recent film work includes *The Playboys*.

SEAMUS DEANE (p. 177)

Poet (*History Lessons*), novelist (*Reading in the Dark*), author (*A Short History of Irish Literature*) and Professor of Modern English and American literature at University College Dublin.

DAME JUDI DENCH (p. 79)

Actor. Acclaimed roles include Cleopatra in *Antony and Cleopatra* at the Royal National Theatre and Mistress Quickly in the film *Henry V*.

THOMAS DOCHERTY (p. 157)

Academic, author (*John Donne, Undone*) and Professor of Modern English at Trinity College Dublin.

MARGARET DRABBLE, CBE (p. 21)

Novelist (*The Millstone, The Radiant Way, A Natural Curiosity, The Gates of Ivory*), biographer (*Arnold Bennett*), lecturer, critic and editor of *The Oxford Companion to English Literature*.

PAUL DURCAN (p. 40)

Poet (*The Berlin Wall Café, Daddy Daddy, Crazy About Women*).

ARCHBISHOP ROBIN EAMES (p. 135)

Archbishop of Armagh and Primate of All Ireland.

BEN ELTON (p. 176)

Comedian, playwright and novelist (*Stark, Gridlock*).

PETER FALLON (p. 130)

Poet (*The First Affair, Winter Work*), editor and founder of The Gallery Press.

ANNE FINE (p. 145)

Novelist primarily for teenagers (*Bill's New Frock, The Granny Project*).

MR JUSTICE THOMAS A. FINLAY (p. 60)

Chief Justice of the Republic of Ireland.

GARRET FITZGERALD (p. 3)

Author (*All in a Life* (autobiography), *Towards a New Ireland*), politician (former Taoiseach and leader of Fine Gael), lecturer and academic.

THEODORA FITZGIBBON (p. 18)

(Deceased) Cookery expert and author.

T. P. FLANAGAN (p. 22)

Artist.

SIR JOHN GIELGUD (p. 58)

Actor. Has played most major roles, most recently Prospero in the film *Prospero's Books*.

ELLEN GILCHRIST (p. 78)

American novelist (*The Anna Papers, Net of Jewels*), short-story writer (*Drunk with Love, I Cannot Get You Close Enough*) and poet (*The Land Surveyor's Daughter*).

HUGO HAMILTON (p. 195)

Novelist (*Surrogate City, The Last Shot*).

SEAMUS HEANEY (p. 30)

Poet (*Death of a Naturalist, Seeing Things*), critic (*Preoccupations: Selected Prose, 1968–1978, The Government of the Tongue*) and professor at Harvard and Oxford.

CHAIM HERZOG (p. 82)

President of Israel.

DESMOND HOGAN (p. 92)

Novelist (*The Leaves on Grey, A Curious Street*) and short-story writer (*The Diamonds at the Bottom of the Sea*).

ALAN HOLLINGHURST (p. 173)

Journalist and novelist (*The Swimming Pool Library*).

MICHAEL HOLROYD (p. 34)

Biographer (*Lytton Strachey, Augustus John, Bernard Shaw*).

MIROSLAV HOLUB (p. 204)

Czechoslovakian poet (*Go and Open the Door, Totally Unsystematic Zoology*) and scientist (*The Dimension of the Present and Other Essays*).

TED HUGHES (p. 1)

Poet Laureate (*Poetry in the Making, The Hawk in the Rain, Lupercal*).

JEREMY IRONS (p. 91)

Actor. Played Charles in the television adaptation of *Brideshead Revisited*. Recent film work includes *Reversal of Fortune* and *Waterland*.

GLENDA JACKSON, MP (p. 149)
Actor (*Stevie*, *A Touch of Class*) and Member of Parliament (Labour Party) representing Hampstead and Highgate.

JENNIFER JOHNSTON (p. 42)
Novelist (*How Many Miles to Babylon?*, *The Invisible Worm*) and playwright.

SR STANISLAUS KENNEDY (p. 76)
Social worker and director of Focus Point.

BRENDAN KENNELLY (p. 9)
Poet (*Cromwell*, *The Book of Judas*) and Professor of English at Trinity College Dublin.

DECLAN KIBERD (p. 186)
Author (*Men and Feminism in Modern Literature*), broadcaster, critic and lecturer in English at University College Dublin.

BENEDICT KIELY (p. 11)
Author, lecturer, broadcaster, novelist (*Proxopera*, *Nothing Happens in Carmincross*), short-story writer (*A Journey to the Severn Streams and Other Stories*) and journalist.

MARY LAVIN (p. 74)
Short-story writer (*Tales from Bective Bridge*, *A Family Likeness*) and novelist (*The House in Clewe Street*).

SUE LAWLEY (p. 191)
Broadcaster and presenter of *Desert Island Discs* on BBC Radio 4.

DAVID LEAVITT (p. 185)
American novelist (*Equal Affections*) and short-story writer (*A Place I've Never Been*).

LAURIE LEE (p. 39)
Writer (*Cider with Rosie*, *As I Walked Out One Midsummer Morning*, *A Moment of War*) and poet (*The Bloom of Candles*).

MARY LELAND (p. 49)
Novelist (*The Killeen*, *Approaching Priests*) and journalist.

HUGH LEONARD (p. 7)
Playwright (*Da*, *A Life*, *Moving*), novelist (*Parnell and the Englishwoman*), author of the autobiographical *Home Before Night* and *Out After Dark* and journalist.

DORIS LESSING (p. 137)
Novelist (*The Grass is Singing*, *The Golden Notebook*) and short-story writer.

DAVID LODGE (p. 109)
Novelist (*Nice Work, Paradise News*), critic (*The Novelist at the Crossroads and Other Essays on Fiction and Criticism*) and Honorary Professor of Modern English Literature at the University of Birmingham.

MICHAEL LONGLEY (p. 158)
Poet (*Man Lying on a Wall, Gorse Fires*).

FERDIA MAC ANNA (p. 141)
Broadcaster, writer (*Bald Head*), television producer and novelist (*The Last of the High Kings*).

MR JUSTICE NIALL MCCARTHY (p. 67)
(Deceased) Supreme Court Judge.

FRANK MCGUINNESS (p. 32)
Playwright (*Observe the Sons of Ulster Marching Towards the Somme, Someone Who'll Watch Over Me*).

SIR IAN MCKELLEN (p. 100)
Actor. Roles include Romeo and Macbeth with the Royal Shakespeare Company and Coriolanus at the Royal National Theatre. Has performed his one-man show *Acting Shakespeare* worldwide.

BERNARD MAC LAVERTY (p. 10)
Novelist (*Cal, Lamb*) and short-story writer (*The Great Profundo and Other Stories*).

BRYAN MACMAHON (p. 112)
Educator and writer of plays, novels (*Children of the Rainbow*) and short stories (*The Lion Tamer, The Red Petticoat*).

DEREK MAHON (p. 43)
Poet (*The Hunt by Night, Antarctica*), translator and anthologist.

SUE MILLER (p. 69)
American novelist (*The Good Mother, Family Pictures*) and short-story writer (*Inventing the Abbotts and Other Stories*).

JOHN MONTAGUE (p. 37)
Poet (*A Chosen Light, The Rough Field*), short-story writer (*Death of a Chieftain*) and visiting professor in America.

CHRISTY MOORE (p. 148)
Singer and songwriter.

ANDREW MOTION (p. 6)
Poet (*The Pleasure Steamers, Love in a Life*), novelist (*The Pale Companion, Famous for the Creatures*), critic and biographer.

DAME IRIS MURDOCH (p. 15)
Novelist (*The Sea, the Sea, The Book and the Brotherhood*), playwright (*The Servants and the Snow*) and philosopher (*The Sovereignty of Good: Metaphysics as a Guide to Morals*).

RICHARD MURPHY (p. 160)
Poet (*High Island, The Price of Stone*) and visiting professor in America.

KEVIN MYERS (p. 64)
Journalist with the *Irish Times*.

EILÉAN NÍ CHUILLEANEÁIN (p. 63)
Poet (*Acts and Monuments, The Magdalene Sermon*) and lecturer in English at Trinity College Dublin.

NUALA NÍ DHOMHNAILL (p. 84)
Poet (*An Dealg Droighin, Selected Poems/Rogha Dánta*).

CONOR CRUISE O'BRIEN (p. 162)
Politician, academic, lecturer, journalist and author (*States of Ireland, God Land: Reflections on Religion and Nationalism*).

JOSEPH O'CONNOR (p. 144)
Novelist (*Cowboys and Indians*) and short-story writer (*True Believers*).

ULICK O'CONNOR (p. 4)
Writer and critic (*Celtic Dawn: A Portrait of the Irish Renaissance, A Terrible Beauty is Born: The Irish Troubles, 1912–1922*).

CARDINAL TOMÁS Ó FIAICH (p. 23)
(Deceased) Cardinal Archbishop of Armagh and church leader.

FINTAN O'TOOLE (p. 51)
Journalist, critic, broadcaster and author (*No More Heroes: A Radical Guide to Shakespeare, A Mass for Jesse James*).

THE RT HON THE LORD OWEN (p. 96)
Politician, founder of the SDP and author of the autobiographical *Time to Declare*.

JAMES PLUNKETT (p. 98)
Novelist (*Strumpet City, Farewell Companions*) and short-story writer (*The Trusting and the Maimed*).

SIR V. S. PRITCHETT (p. 140)
Novelist (*Clare Drummer*), critic and short-story writer (*When My Girl Comes Home, The Camberwell Beauty and Other Stories*).

CHRISTOPHER RICKS (p. 151)
Scholar, author (*Milton's Grand Style*) and Professor of English at Boston University.

PERMISSIONS

JOHN ASHBERY: Carcanet Press for 'Crazy Weather'.

W. H. AUDEN: Faber & Faber for 'A Summer Night', 'Petition' and 'The More Loving One' from *W. H. Auden: Collected Poems*, edited by Edward Mendelson.

GEORGE BARKER: Faber & Faber for 'Summer Song I' from *Collected Poems*.

HILAIRE BELLOC: The Peters Fraser & Dunlop Group for 'The Death and Last Confession of Wandering Peter'.

ELIZABETH BISHOP: Farrar, Straus & Giroux for 'The Moose' from *The Complete Poems 1927–1979*, copyright © 1979, 1983 by Alice Helen Methfessel.

CHARLES BUKOWSKI: Black Sparrow Press, California, for 'Rock', copyright © 1981, reprinted from *Dangling in the Tournefortia*.

RAYMOND CARVER: HarperCollins Publishers for 'Happiness'.

PAUL CELAN: John Johnson for 'Psalm', translated by Michael Hamburger.

HART CRANE: Liveright Publishing Corporation for the extract from 'Voyages', reprinted from *The Collected Poems and Selected Letters and Prose of Hart Crane*, copyright © 1933, 1958, 1966, by Liveright Publishing Corporation.

CYRIL CUSACK: Colin Smythe, Bucks, for 'Confiteor'.

MICHAEL DAVITT: Raven Arts Press for 'An Scáthán'; Faber & Faber for Paul Muldoon's translation of 'The Mirror' from *Quoof* by Paul Muldoon.

D. J. ENRIGHT: Watson, Little for 'Biography' from *Paradise Illustrated*.

SERGEI ESSENIN: Macmillan for Gordon McVay's translation of 'My Teper' Ukhodim Ponemnogu' from *Isadora and Esenin* (1980).

ROBERT FROST: The Estate of Robert Frost and Jonathan Cape for 'The Road Not Taken' and 'Stopping by Woods on a Snowy Evening'.

ELLEN GILCHRIST: Don Congdon Associates for 'Shut Up, I'm Going to Sing You a Love Song'.

INDEX OF POETS AND THEIR WORKS

INDEX OF FIRST LINES